praise for
lessons from the ledge

Nancy Nelson's *Lessons from the Ledge* takes us on her journey through a tragedy that no one would want to experience. Her raw, transparent and authentic writing walks us through that experience with her, teaching us how to navigate our own life-ledge moments. Our family experienced the dark depths of loss after losing our first daughter to Pompe's disease. I know the view from the ledge all too well.
—Wendy Franz, Designer

With unflinching candor, Nancy Nelson shares her complex story of grief and loss. Unable to protect her children from the pain and sorrow brought on by her soon-to-be ex-husband's suicide, she digs deep spiritually on her journey from shock to healing. Anyone whose suffered loss will relate to this book, and, in particular, widowed moms will benefit from Nelson's honesty and wisdom.
—Heidi Kronenberg LCSW, Director of Operations at ESME.com

One of my closest and dearest friends, Nancy Jo Nelson shares her journey of dealing with and overcoming a horrible tragedy that could have left her hopeless. For anyone who is trying to deal with tragedy, grief and loss, *Lessons From the Ledge* provides hope and encouragement that there is a way to heal, forgive, and regain control of life.
—Joe Pulio, Teacher at Lake Forest High School

The hard-learned lessons Nancy Nelson shares throughout the book on guilt, forgiveness, grief, self-love, and joy are life-changing. Your "mess" is now your "message" and one that the world definitely needs to hear.
—Gail Brown, President/Founder of Engaging Speakers

lessons from the ledge

a memoir by

Nancy Jo Nelson

Stonebrook Publishing
Saint Louis, MO

A STONEBROOK PUBLISHING BOOK
Copyright © 2017 by Nancy Jo Nelson
All rights reserved.
Edited by Nancy Erickson, TheBookProfessor
The BookProfessor.com
All rights reserved. Published in the United States by Stonebrook Publishing, a division of Stonebrook Enterprises, LLC, Saint Louis, Missouri. No part of this book may be reproduced, scanned, or distributed in any printed or electronic form without written permission from the author.

Cover Design by Blank Slate Communications
Cover Image: Shutterstock

Definitions 1 and 2 of "Ledge" from Dictionary.com

Please do not participate in or encourage piracy of copyrighted materials in violation of the authors' rights.
Library of Congress Control Number: 2017937429

ISBN: 978-1-7347340-2-7
www.stonebrookpublishing.net

PRINTED IN THE UNITED STATES OF AMERICA
10 9 8 7 6 5 4 3 2 1

He walked in the door holding a shoe with a sock still inside, a scrap of plaid, and a sunglass lens. "I can't believe they left this there. He was a person!"

lessons from the ledge

i.

Ledge: noun

A relatively narrow, projecting part, as a horizontal, shelf-like projection on a wall or a raised edge on a tray

A more or less flat shelf of rock protruding from a cliff or slope

The place you live when life is out of control, scary, or unpredictable

Ledges. We've all been on them. If you haven't, you're either a liar, dead, or very, very lucky. Usually loss puts us on it: loss of a job, a relationship, a death, our direction, our identity, our health, our security. Loss puts us there. Fear keeps us there. Stuck.

I've learned. A lot.

This story is from my heart to yours. On a cellular level, my hope is that when you're done reading, you will feel like we're friends. Friends who relate to ledges and reinforce each other, so the next ledge—and there will be one—is less scary.

Take what you need from these ledge lessons and do your ledge better. Do your life on the ground better, too.

Learn to love the view from wherever you are.

> Life is a quest, not a journey.
> —Sir Ken Richardson, Ph.D

There is only one world, the world pressing against you at this minute. There is only one minute in which you are alive, this minute here and now. The only way to live is by accepting each minute as an unrepeatable miracle.
—Storm Jameson

1

Ah … Garbage Day. He stood there with the bag in his hand.

We're navigating this divorce thing really well, I thought as Jill and I headed out to the car. No angry outbursts, no heated arguments. The opposite of love is not hate. It is indifference. And that's why I was done.

I'm so done, I need a new word for done.

Wrangling Jill to school on Wednesday, October 7th, 2009, I talked to Bob over my shoulder as we were on our way out. "Have a good day. I'll call you later from work to see what you figured out about the house."

The bank needed proof that I could afford my next-step-of-my-life condo. It was time to talk about splitting our home.

Eighteen head-banging years against the Bob-wall were coming to an end. Relief washed over me, and I could finally picture a new future without the struggles or the exhaustion of trying so hard to be heard and seen.

My heart was with Keith now, and that made me feel strong, supported, and even invincible. I was reclaiming my power, and it felt really, really good.

Around noon, I called Bob for a financial update. No answer. Not unusual.

After school, Sam called me at work. "Hey Mom! I figured out the coolest feature on my phone!"

"Awesome, Dude! Did you tell Dad?" I asked.

"No," he said. "He's not here."

That was odd. Bob was always home when Sam burst through the door after school. It was a perk of working for himself from home. Every day. Like clockwork, and even more so now that I had a job AND had apparently lost my mind.

Hours passed. No Bob. No call. I began to wonder and worry.

When Sam's hockey practice time came and went, but Bob didn't, I got more worried. The kids were getting anxious and scared. They came with me to my indoor soccer game, so we could stick together. At halftime, the kids were staring from the stands, clearly concerned, so I called home again.

"This isn't funny anymore," I yelled into the answering machine. "You NEED to call me!"

We arrived home to an empty house. Bob always left a note on one of his hand-cut pieces of scrap paper, so I went down to his office in the basement to check if there was a note. But there was nothing. Now the kids were really upset.

"Mom, you have to call the police! Something is seriously wrong." Jill was pale and concerned.

At her insistence, I dialed 911 but felt like I shouldn't.

"He's a grown man, Jill, and there's usually a forty-eight hour waiting period before a person is considered missing. I feel like an idiot!" I hissed, waiting for the police to answer.

As soon as the dispatcher answered, I jumped in, almost cutting her off. "Hi, my name is Nancy Nelson, and my husband has been missing all day. I know this seems a little crazy since he hasn't been gone that long, but something just feels wrong."

"Are there any unusual circumstances?" the dispatcher asked. "Any family or personal issues?"

"Well, he's a recovering alcoholic, and we're going through a divorce. His mom has cancer. His car is here, his wallet is here, his cell phone is here, and his bike is here. Nothing is missing, except for him."

"We'll send some officers over, ma'am. They'll be there shortly."

I went back to the basement to recheck his desk. Maybe I'd missed something. There was nothing on his calendar. The checkbook was in the usual place. I flipped it open to see if there were any withdrawals that would provide a clue, and a piece of paper fluttered out. I picked it up and stared—it was a deposit slip for $17,500, the same amount as my annual salary. It had today's date on it. Bob had written the check from his business account that morning. Bile rose in my throat, and I felt the blood drain from my face.

Bob was meticulous about everything, especially our finances, but he'd just stuck this deposit slip in the checkbook. This from a guy who kept a tally of how many pens were in a box, marking any change to the total with hash marks lined up like soldiers. He would never *forget* to write a $17,500 deposit in our check register. He would never put that amount of money into an account I could access, because he trusted no one but himself.

Police cars pulled up to our house, their red and blue lights spinning into the neighbors' windows. Officers. Dogs. It was a nightmare. Reggie, the detective assigned to our case, introduced himself. He was from the sheriff's office and asked if he could have something of Bob's to give the search team. I rifled through the clothes hamper and offered one of Bob's t-shirts to the search dogs. After the search team left, Reggie flipped open a notebook and told me to tell him about the events of the day.

"Better spill it about Keith, Mom!" Jill said with righteous fury.

Drowning in shame, I gave him Keith's address and phone number. He was now a "person of interest."

When things got really hard in my marriage and

my frustration and pain hit record highs, I would often wonder where Keith was. He had taken me to my junior prom, and we were a couple, off and on, for ten years. Keith loved the *real* me with all he had. Our relationship had been deep, intense, and beyond our maturity level at the time. We were like magnets, attract and repel, repel and attract. But it was too soon and too much for us back then.

Keith showed up again right after I'd met Bob, but there was no more room for him. Bob was my man, and all my energy went to him. My focus was on my future—one that I hoped I would spend with Bob. Forever. With the on and off, intense chemistry of our past relationship, I knew I'd sabotage "Bob world" if Keith hung around. So I asked him to leave, and he fell off the face of the earth.

But happily ever after with Bob never happened.

Twenty years later, I stood in the shower and prayed, "God, help me let go of Keith. You know where he is and that needs to be enough. This is ridiculous. I can't wonder and wish forever. I'm married to Bob, and I have to work at the relationship I'm in now. It's time to let Keith go."

The next day, the day before Father's Day, Keith found me on Facebook.

I had no explanation for this other than divine intervention. I was trying to let go. Not hold on.

I ran down the stairs that day and blurted to my family, "Guess who just found me on Facebook? Keith!"

I didn't hide anything but the significance of the timing.

We began to message each other to fill in the years. His life in Oregon. My life and family at home. By our third message, "I love you and always have" was our sign off. We went very deep very fast. The pain and hurt and frustration of my eighteen-year marriage spilled out. Lost in the desert and dying of thirst for so long, Keith reminded me who I was pre-Bob. During my Bob years, I morphed into someone I barely recognized. I was blurry. I was compromised. I was fake. I was done. Keith was the catalyst, not the cause. I had been unhappy and frustrated and angry and sad for years.

Keith remembered me from before. Before I sanded myself down. Before I blended into the mundane. Before my self-perception warped. And then I remembered. I finally felt my "fed up." So much of me was gone, hidden, dead. The contrast between his memories of me and my reality was undeniable. Finally.

I had tried to leave Bob when Sam was a baby. Bob figured it was a phase and I'd snap out of it. My low self-esteem made me believe I was unemployable, unlovable, and incapable, so I stayed. And I worked on myself. I changed my thinking from "I'm trapped" to "I'm making the choice every day to stay."

Keith understood me. On a level no one else ever had. We had been through so much all those years ago. I had stayed with his little sister so he could be at the hospital with his mom as she died from cancer. Stood by his side at the funeral. An indelible imprint at a horrendous time. We had a past, and now we had a present. He had walked many of the same egg-shelled rooms in his marriage house before his recent divorce. He'd also tried to leave his marriage before he ultimately broke free. He understood how hard it was to get to this final point and told me he'd understand if I decided to stay, but wouldn't judge if I couldn't. After all the years in "the desert," I gulped down every word of his messages to quench my thirst.

"Tell me all the things you want." Keith's question hit a nerve buried under years of dead expectations in the box Bob created. I had to dig before I could answer. *"I want to be seen, heard, and understood."* Bob couldn't, so I had no sense of self in the warped reflection he mirrored for me. He couldn't validate me, so I felt unvalued by him, so he felt unvalued by me. I gave Bob my power but didn't realize it wasn't his job to be my mirror. But Keith saw, heard, and understood me and helped me remember. Keith helped me to see myself, instead of a reflected image. The hard work of my resurrection had begun.

I gave Keith my heart and he guarded it with a passion I never experienced. I wrote and spoke my deepest needs to Oregon and knew they were heard, understood, and treasured. He loved me enough to see me reemerge with no expectations of a future with me. In the safety of the miles between us, I began to unravel the years and reveal the real me.

Less than a month after Keith found me, I pulled up a chair across the table from Bob. He was eating lunch.

"I need to talk to you," I said. "We both know we aren't happy, and we haven't been for a very long time. I want a divorce, and it's not because of Keith."

His fork stopped midair. The food spilled from it. He blinked a couple of times but said nothing. My stomach knotted from a mixture of profound sadness and unspeakable relief. I'd finally said the words, words that had been pent up inside for years. Silence hung over the table.

"You don't know what you're doing," he whispered.

"I'm sorry, but I can't be ME with you," I said gently. "We can do this with a mediator to keep the costs down. It doesn't have to be ugly."

Bob put down his fork, stood up from the table, and cleared his plate. A rare occurrence. End of conversation.

So there it was. I was relieved. I was excited. I was scared. All at once. And in that moment, Bob was right. I didn't know what I was doing, and I'm so glad I didn't.

As days became weeks, I wrapped myself in the safe cocoon of Keith with a vengeance. We texted each other and kept up our Facebook messages. We talked on the phone whenever I was out of the house. We gulped each other down, raced forward, and discussed our fears and hopes.

Bob sensed something had shifted in me this time. Keith was the permission I'd needed to do what was inevitable. I pushed Bob to make an appointment with a mediator so we could move forward with the divorce. I promised I would help him take care of his mom as she battled cancer. I knew he had a lot on his plate, and I was sorry to add to it, but I had to take care of myself. For once. For finally.

When it was time to tell Jillian, sixteen, and Sam, eleven, I did it alone because Bob was busy sailing down the river "Denial." There'd be no dramatic announcement by us together. No scripted scene like the movies. Emotional issues were not his area. I figured it wouldn't be a complete surprise and that after years of watching me struggle, they might be relieved or even happy for me. Yeah, right.

I told them separately. It sucked. They were angry. And sad. And I was wrong. They were neither relieved nor happy for me. I wished I could have a do-over. When I told friends and family, no one was surprised. One friend asked, "What took you so long?" It was no secret that we struggled. It was no secret I hurt. It was no secret my hurt had turned to anger. Many of these people had prayed for us and offered comfort and advice on how to stay the course. Until I couldn't anymore. I finally waved the white flag of surrender.

The night Bob disappeared, Jill's two best friends came over and helped her make a huge sign they taped on our garage door:

OK, Dad. It's Not Funny Anymore. Joke's Over. Come Home.

Sam sat in the family room by himself and played video games. We all just tried to remember to breathe. Keith waited in Oregon. Unable to do a thing.

Angry at my fall from grace, Jill shut me out. She wouldn't talk to me, but Sam clung. Thursday night as he and I lay in bed and listened to the rain, he asked "Mom? Do you think Dad's safe out there?"

"Dad is smart, Sam, and I'm sure he's somewhere safe and dry. He's got to try to figure stuff out. Besides, his shotgun is still downstairs," I reassured.

Sam piped up. "Mom, he has two: his single barrel from when he was a kid and the double barrel one from Papa. He showed it to me on Sunday as he cleaned it. He let me hold it. It's really heavy."

Holy shit! I shot out of bed and went down to the basement again. The gun wasn't there. My dad's double-barrel shotgun. I phoned the detective.

"Hi, Reggie. It's Nancy Nelson. I'm sorry to call you so late, but we just discovered that a shotgun is missing. I thought you might need to know."

Missing ARMED man. New scenario. New case. New fear.

The first few days were a blur as I told and retold the story to people who called to check in. I guess I ate. I know I slept a little. I guess the kids ate. I don't think Jill slept. Maybe Sam did. One friend camped out on my couch. Another, my "Love You Like A Sister Without

Baggage" friend, came to be with me in the chaos, fear, and shock. Still another rushed over to hold me tight as I tried to digest all of this.

Jill broke wide open, but Sam shrank. Every day we hunkered down in this new family foxhole. With a broken daughter and shrunken son, it was an unfixable situation for the fixer-mom. Caused by the fixer-mom?

On Friday, the cadaver dogs came. The search team and their dogs had combed the area for a trail the day he left. Nothing. So now cadaver dogs. *Cadaver* dogs.

They dragged the nearby river to look for Bob's body. Police went door to door. Asked questions. There was no privacy. Looks of pity burned into me at the grocery store. We felt naked and exposed at the bus stop as Sam soldiered up the stairs and into his seat, a kid who wanted to return to a normal that no longer existed. Faces pressed against the windows, eager to see what tragedy looked like.

And then there were the comments. Underneath the news articles about the Barrington Man's disappearance were plenty of online comments.

"Check his Swiss bank account."

"No, there's probably no money. I drove by his house. It's kind of shabby."

"Ask his girlfriend. There must be a girlfriend."

Like playground bullies, these people forgot that there were people involved. Real people. Real children. A real family.

By Saturday, our house was full. My cousin came from Iowa, and Bob's best friend was in from Michigan. Jill's friends were all around, too. Bob's mom sat quietly, a little knit hat on her bald chemo head. Pseudo shiva sitting. It was like a wake, but not really. The chitchat was awkward as we waited for news and waited for Bob. Keith remained in Oregon, helplessly glued to his phone and frustrated he couldn't be present for me to lean on. But he was the scapegoat. Because it was easier to blame a stranger than to blame a mom.

This was not in the damn life brochure. What should I say? What do I do?

I bought Sam a bike.

The ever-present Detective Reggie stood out, a black man in a sea of white. A fixture in my home now. He watched. He listened. He interviewed Bob's best friend, John, who told him stories about Bob's past that I'd never known or long forgotten and buried deep, things like Bob's alias and illegal driver's license.

"Didn't you think this would be pertinent information for me to know, Nancy?" Reggie accused.

Shit. I didn't need this. Not now. A whole lifetime had passed since that drama, and it was tucked way back in my brain. Jill and Sam knew nothing about their dad's alcohol-soaked life before they were born. They'd rarely even seen him drink a non-alcoholic beer, and we kept no alcohol in our house. So, of course, I hadn't mentioned his alias and past. After all, it wasn't him anymore. And it wasn't my story to tell.

"I've never had a missing husband before," I shot back. "I don't know what I'm doing here!" I took a deep breath to steady myself. "Do I need a lawyer?"

We'd been seeing a therapist, and he showed up at the house, too. Role reversal. Blindsided by his missing client, he was shaken to his therapist core.

"What did I miss?" he whispered on the verge of tears. "I didn't anticipate any of this. I'm so sorry."

"That's okay," I assured him. "Nobody knows Bob. Nobody."

I had tried to be patient. I had let Bob process the divorce in his own way and in his own time. But as weeks turned to months, he'd dug in his heels. He asked me to go to counseling, something I'd begged him to do countless times over countless years. I agreed.

"But only if the goal is to figure out how to be the best co-parents possible. Not reconciliation." My terms this time.

He read *The Love Dare* at my cousin's suggestion and tried to do all the assignments in the book. To check off the tasks and create a miraculous reconciliation if he just followed the directions. Thirty days of little niceties, favors, and notes to restore more than eighteen years of damage, scars, and hurt. Far too little far too late.

He lasted seventeen days before he admitted he

wasn't any good at finishing stuff. He couldn't change his behavior. He only did what the book told him to because the book told him to do it. He could only ever go through the motions. Nothing more.

I. Was. Done.

In our first session, the therapist confirmed what he thought Bob needed to hear—that I was headed down a dead end with Keith. It was unlikely that my relationship with Keith would work. He'd seen this before.

I sat there and shook my head. *You didn't hear one word I said. I sat here and told you our entire marriage history. I've never been saner in my life! Don't you get it? It's NOT about Keith, you idiot! It's about* **enough**. *I've had* **enough**, *and I AM* **enough**.

Bob and I grabbed a cup of coffee after the second session.

"Honestly, Bob, I'm so sorry," I said. "I will totally support you while you figure things out. I'm the last person who'd judge you. You will grow a lot. I'll always love you, and I'll do whatever I can to help with your mom. And I'm not even closed to the idea of a new future with you. I have no idea where we're headed, but our past can't be fixed. We need a clean break. An end to this. Our marriage is dead, and it needs to be buried so a new, better way of life can take root and grow for both of us. We will always be connected by our amazing kids, and I want us to be the best parents we can be," I explained. "I can even picture calling to invite you to have dinner with us."

I felt so damn progressive and was certain that no one else would ever have such a warm, affectionate, balanced divorce. *We'll be best friends, great divorced parents, and amazing evolved human beings. We'll both be happier!*

Our poor therapist was so flustered by Bob's disappearance that when he got to our house that day, he locked his keys in his car. When he tried to leave and realized he was keyless, he waited for help outside in the chill instead of coming back in. I don't blame him. The house was a hard place to wait.

The weekend came and went with no news, and life moved forward. It had to. Columbus Day on Monday—a day off for breathing space. It was obvious Jill needed help. Help that I couldn't give and that she didn't want from me anyway. She spun out of control, consumed by her grief and shock and anger. She hated me. I was afraid she would hurt someone. Or herself. Her pain was so big and raw. She couldn't sleep. She didn't eat. There was no safety. There was no buffer. Our family and friends felt it.

Back in July when Jill learned about the divorce, she told Bob she wanted to live with him. Not with me. She pledged allegiance to her dad. And now that he was gone, she was abandoned to the enemy. We fought. We cried. We tiptoed around each other and tried to find our way forward. But the divorce and Bob's disappearance could not have happened at a worse time in her life, and that broke my heart. She was so vulnerable, and her relationship with her dad had gotten messy lately because she felt he didn't hear her. Or see her. Or understand her. She felt neither of us did. But I understood. She had yelled at her dad the night before he disappeared because he hadn't answered his phone when she'd needed a ride home from Bible study. Now she blamed herself.

"Why wasn't the fact that I wanted to live with him enough to make Dad stay?"

An unanswerable question.

In one short/very long week, I learned how hard it is to watch your child suffer. I also learned how important it is to get the right help for them—no matter how difficult the decisions.

And what was the icing on my shit cake? Exhausted after all the insurance hassles and intake paperwork, not to mention the stress and deep, gut-wrenching anxiety of checking my baby girl into a hospital because I feared she was falling apart, I headed home. I wanted to be with Sam. I needed to be with him. I just wanted to go to sleep and escape this nightmare. And there were my keys, locked in my van. Alone in the dark in the hospital parking lot, I laughed and cried at the irony, and expected them to come out with a straitjacket to admit me.

Life had changed in an instant of eight days of hell.

2

I met Bob at a '50s costume party in 1989. I'd just been dumped by an attorney and had sworn off dating. Bob was dressed as a nerd, and I was a sweater girl à la Lana Turner, wearing angora that clung and showed off my "assets." When he and his best friend, John, walked in, they saw me on the dance floor as I was tossed around like a rag doll by a very tall partygoer. John pointed to me and said, "You're going to marry that girl, Bobby." Bob followed John's point and said, "Hey, I know her from high school. That's Nancy Strickland."

Bob was a charmer, and we shared that high school connection, which was huge for me because high school had been such a special time in my life. We knew tons of the same people. We had walked the same halls, had the same teachers, experienced many of the same things—all conversation starters.

We danced and laughed. And laughed some more. We had some serious chemistry. At the end of the evening,

Bob said we should go out sometime, so I asked if he wanted my number.

"Are you in the phone book?" Nicely played, Bob, nicely played. Casual. Confident.

"Well, yeah …" I tried to match his casual confidence.

"I'll find you then." As he turned to saunter away, I called after him.

"Wait, this isn't going to be one of those 'I'll call you' things and then you don't, is it?"

He looked back over his shoulder and said, "This isn't going to be one of those 'I call you and you don't remember me' things, is it?"

Whoa … this guy could go head to head with me. And he was funny. It was so sexy. Quick wit. Great delivery. Attractive. Chemistry. I was hooked.

On our first date, I told Bob, "I want to be a housewife and mother like in the '50s. I want to be Donna Reed."

Okay, maybe I wouldn't actually vacuum in pearls and high heels, but other than that, I'd be a perfect imitation of her. And my mom. Perfect house. Perfect meals. Perfect kids. If that wasn't what Bob wanted, at least we'd know right off the bat and wouldn't waste our time.

It WAS what Bob wanted. He wanted me. My mom wanted that life *for* me, and it really was what I believed I wanted. I had internalized my mother's story and had made it mine. I owned her story. It was so big and vivid and tragic. The line between where she ended and I began was blurred.

Our attraction was instantaneous and ferocious. We were the perfect couple, based on our family histories. Bob was different from all the other guys I'd dated, and yet he was the perfect combination of all their best parts. He had a dry sense of humor, was nice to everyone, and could work a room. He was close to his family and had a good job in his father's business. He was ready to settle down. He made me feel attractive and loved. He looked like he belonged, and he fit in my family. He was a grown-up.

And he was an alcoholic.

I imitated my mom in my life and relationships. Like a dutiful, trained monkey, I mirrored and reflected her until I *was* her, until I validated her life and choices with my own life and choices. That was our covert and defining rule. Imitation is the highest form of flattery, and she needed me to fill the gigantic wound from her story. But that "rule" felt unpredictable. Just like loving and living with an alcoholic was unpredictable. Always off balance. Always on guard. Rules set, broken, and reset again.

On July 4th, after fourteen months in Bob's teeter-totter world of alcoholism, he proposed to me on a boat in the middle of beautiful Walloon Lake in Northern Michigan, where his family had a cottage. "So if you say 'no,' you have to swim back," he joked. It was a perfect afternoon. The sky was filled with God clouds; rays of sun peeked through, like fingers of His giant hand that reached down to touch us.

I wasn't surprised. He had asked my dad for his permission and blessing to marry me the weekend before, and my dad had called to give me a play by play.

"It's about time!" he'd told Bob. "And we hugged. Then I sat him down for a long talk about his drinking," Dad said, "and how it never made anything better in a marriage. I wanted him to hear it from me as his future father-in-law. Because I know."

Nine months later, wearing my mother-in-law's wedding gown since she didn't have a daughter and my mom didn't have a wedding gown for me to wear, and with my eyes wide open, I became Mrs. Robert D. Nelson. The wedding train of youth and love and hope sped down the wedding track, drowned out my doubts, and silenced my gut. I had muffled my intuition my whole life. It was buried so deeply, I could hardly hear a murmur. But God's voice got through loud and clear. As I listened to my cousins rehearse their music before the ceremony, I felt God say "Don't worry, Nance. I've got this. He'll be sober in a year."

With His assurance, I walked down that aisle and said my vows and smiled and danced and celebrated with a hopeful heart in a room full of people who cared about me and the man I loved.

For better or worse, I became "wife" that day.

I also became "The Alcoholism Expert," able to leap tall buildings of addiction and rivers of denial in a single bound! And I'd already had plenty of practice on that score.

lessons from the ledge

Fake It 'Til You Make It. That's what you learn when you grow up in an alcoholic home. Pretend. Put on the face. Paste on a smile and look good. Keep up the appearance that your family is "normal" and predictable and looks like the American dream. Pretend to know what the American dream and normal and predictable look like. Sit in the back pew at church on Sunday morning and try not to smell the gin that seeped out of your father's skin. Smile. Hand over all control and emotion to a broken man who struggles, limps along, and does the best he can.

Alcoholic dynamics are a bitch to navigate. Even if the days of sobriety begin to add up, the old family behaviors continue. As a child, we were never the family at support groups or therapy, and we didn't talk about "It." We didn't know about codependency. We all just did the best we could to survive and even, sometimes, to thrive.

If Dad didn't drink, my mom didn't get angry. If he did, she did. There was no predictability or pattern, rhyme or reason. Sometimes he would stop before he got drunk and sometimes he didn't. I asked him why.

"You know, Nance, I wish I knew. Sometimes I can have a couple of drinks like everyone else. Sometimes it's like I'm headed over the falls in a barrel, and I can't stop."

He couldn't look me in the eye. His shame was so very deep, and his honesty broke my heart.

Fake it 'til you make it. Bury your gut instinct. Stuff your anger down because it's ugly, and no one wants to be around ugly. Don't bring shame to the family name. Keep up appearances.

Appearances of what? A normal family? What is normal anyway? My mom didn't know. I didn't know. Nobody knew. But I did know one thing: dads weren't supposed to be drunk.

These are the lessons I learned when I grew up, and I carried them into my own home. Our home. The Bob and Nancy Nelson home. Engrained patterns of behavior that we played out as we dated and when we married. Familiar knee-jerk reactions and those unhealthy expectations, like toilet paper stuck to my shoe.

3

Bob got sober the first December we were married, just like God had promised right before I walked down the aisle in April. He came home from a hunting trip up north and called Alcoholics Anonymous (AA). He literally walked in the door and picked up the phone.

I'd already left him once after an out-all-night-no-phone-call episode.

I think Bob thought he was getting sober for himself, but he really did it for me. And he knew it was something he *should* do.

But alcoholics must overcome their addiction for themselves, not for anyone else. It's terrifying and courageous and is a hard, slippery fight. It alters their lives and rocks their worlds as sobriety rips away years of dishonesty. It can even heal current generations and those to come. But it's a battle.

My new role of "Best Supportive Sobriety Wife" started immediately. The "Alcoholism Expert" cape, so comfortable and familiar from all the years of wear and tear, was now worn and threadbare. I had memorized all the verses to the "alcoholic family victim song" when I was a child. But this was new. How was I to *act* with a **sober** husband?

New lyrics. New Tune.

But I was a fast learner, and my eyes were wide open when I fell in love and married Bob. I knew he was an alcoholic and that the odds were stacked against us. Growing up in an alcoholic home, the odds are high that you either marry one or become one. Sometimes both.

I threw myself into my new role. My weekly Al-Anon meetings seemed foreign, yet required. The fact that my husband was a ***recovering*** alcoholic mentally separated me from the others who still lived with an active drinker. I wore my rose-colored glasses to every meeting and was so grateful, so *blessed* I wasn't in their shoes. They did their twelve-step work, while I played along. After all, I must have already done the hard work because Bob was now sober.

Years earlier, I had learned in Adult Children of Alcoholics (ACOA) that the work never ends, but somehow I forgot this. Codependency got the best of me. Again.

I always knew that alcohol was never the core issue. It was simply the means to muffle the voice of "I'm not good enough." Alcohol was the chosen substance to numb that pain and place the blame, but when alcohol moved out, something else moved in: control. In Bob's case, he tried to control everything and everyone outside himself, in order to feel okay and good enough inside.

It takes a tremendous amount of work and bravery to change that "not good enough" message. Big bravery to do the hard work, feel the hurt, and release the anger. But as hard as Bob tried, he couldn't do it. And he knew he couldn't, which added insult to injury. He already felt "not good enough" and now he was a failure at the work to figure out why. Even though he tried so hard. Or maybe *because* he was trying so hard and still failed.

No matter how much I loved him, he couldn't love himself.

God grant me the serenity
to accept the things I cannot change;
courage to change the things I can;
and wisdom to know the difference.

That prayer demanded more from Bob than he could give. Serenity to accept what he couldn't change, courage to change, and wisdom to know which was which. Tricky and hard. So much work. So much effort. No matter how much I told him and showed him every day that I loved him and was proud of him, he couldn't receive or believe it. I showered him with words of affirmation. I treated him like I yearned to be treated. But my actions couldn't penetrate his hardened "I'm not good enough" shell. No matter how hard he tried to open himself up.

But he did try.

Bob worked AA *his way*, and when he'd been sober for ten years, he came home from one of his twice-a-year trips up north. In the fall, he and his best friend would hunt, and in the spring, they'd fish. He confessed to me that he not only drank on that trip, but that he had binged. He felt like he deserved it because he was "so good" all the rest of the year. No one needed to be the wiser. Until they got busted for DUI. His friend wouldn't let him drive since Bob had a wife and kids. So the friend took the hit.

My first thought was, *I'm not crazy!* In my gut I'd felt like something was "off" about those trips, but I had thought it was just me. That Bob couldn't wait to get away from me, and that he hated coming home. To me. And he let me think that. But it was really his guilty conscience. And his hangover. My second thought was, *Everyone falls off the wagon. It's okay. We'll get through this.*

When Bob said, "Nancy, I've been doing this for years. These were premeditated binges," I thought something entirely different. *How dare you let me think it was about me all these years? You are a liar. This is NOT love!*

But we worked through it. My dad was dying, and we had a life and children together. So I forgave him, and things were really good between us. For six whole months in a row. I got three months of good after each baby was born and six months of good this time. A whopping total of twelve months sprinkled amongst seventeen years. Sobriety is hard work.

But he did try. We both did.

4

I lost my voice. I surrendered my power. Soon after we were married I handed both over to Bob, along with the financial reins. I didn't know how much money Bob earned when we got married. Maybe he'd told me back then, but I soon forgot. And after Jill was born, I felt like it was none of my business. I was Mom now.

This transformation to voiceless, powerless wife happened at breakneck speed once I had a child. The submissive wife role came directly and indirectly from my mother. It's what I thought I wanted. It's what I was shown I wanted. Except my story wasn't the same as hers. Somewhere deep inside, I knew it shouldn't fit me. And yet, I made it fit. I forced myself to fit into my mother's expectations for my life, like the stepsisters tried to cram their feet into Cinderella's shoe. I knew it and I hated it, so I hated me.

"You're nothing without a man. He's the breadwinner. He does the 'math part' of life. That's his job." My mom's spoken and unspoken words and her own lifestyle example were etched into my mind.

"Take care of everyone else. EVERY. ONE. ELSE."

That's the battle cry of so many women. Until one day, you lose your mind because you've lost yourself. Until one day, when everyone takes advantage of you "doing everything for them" without a word of thanks, you snap. Until one day, everyone takes you for granted because you do everything invisibly. Their appreciation of your "self-less" selfishness does not match your level of self-sacrifice. And then, you can no longer continue.

I learned that script from my mom. She passed it on like a ghost story around the campfire, and it defined my whole family. And it defined me as her daughter.

For years, I tried to:
- Have dinner on the table every night at 6:00 p.m.
- Remember the napkins.
- Wait to call Bob for dinner until the napkins were on the table.
- Make kick-ass Halloween costumes. Cheaply.
- Entertain graciously. Cheaply.
- Volunteer at school.
- Cook from scratch. Cheaply.
- Make every moment count.
- Be teachable.
- Wear a smile.

- Look as good as possible. Cheaply.
- Never leave the house without mascara.
- See the good in Bob.
- Remember the fun times and laughs.
- Focus on what a great dad he became.
- Bury the pain of disconnection and emotional distance.
- Quiet the voice that said something was wrong with me because he couldn't love me.

And yet, despite everything I did for others, I felt invisible. Even to me. Years of frustration. Gallons of tears. I yearned to be real. I ached to be seen, even as big and small parts of me died over the years and the marriage illusion played on. Many. Hard. Years. Of. Fake.

We'd sit down for dinner and if the napkins were not in place, Bob would pantomime wiping his face. Not ask. Not remind. Not get up from the table and get them himself. But pantomime. As my children watched and learned and wondered why their dad couldn't use his words.

If Bob heard no footsteps on the floor above his basement desk, he'd pop upstairs from his office and check on me. If I was off my feet for even a second, he'd ask, "Don't you have something to do?"

When I told him my friend's cancer had returned and I just needed him to hug me for a second, he said, "I can't always do what you want me to do." He walked away. I stood frozen and stunned. All I wanted was comfort and reassurance. All I wanted was a hug. From my husband. What was wrong with *me* that I wasn't worthy of a simple embrace? A slap in my face would have hurt less.

But I didn't give up. I prayed. I vented to friends. I asked my therapist what I could do to fix the relationship. I blamed myself. I internalized my pain and kept on smiling. I hoped and hoped and hoped again that he would love me. I let down my guard so many times, only to be sucker punched again. But I trusted it would get better. Had to get better. I tiptoed around our issues and tried to do everything "right" in Bob's eyes. Until I couldn't anymore. Because nothing got better. No matter how hard I tried. If ten things were right and one was wrong, I heard about my error. There was no acknowledgment of the ten "right" things.

So after eighteen years, I finally asked Bob, "What do we have here? The kids are growing up fast and won't need us forever. We don't share any hobbies. We don't like the same things. I don't even think you like me. When the kids are grown and we're retired, what will that look like? What are we doing?"

"Well, I just figured we'd put our relationship on the shelf until the kids were raised." His unemotional response was no surprise, and that broken-hearted, trapped, itchy sensation washed over me like a familiar tidal wave until I couldn't breathe. That's it? That's all I get? Like our marriage was a dented can at the grocery store? Stuck on a shelf in the back until there's nothing else left to eat? Dangerous thoughts entered my mind as I drove, like *If I swerved in front of that truck and died, maybe he'd realize all I do. Maybe then he'd understand my value to the family. Maybe then he'd see me for who I am. Who I was. Maybe he'd miss me.* But then two beautiful faces would flash in front of me, and I knew I would never do that to my kids.

This wasn't how marriage was supposed to be. We were broken. All the years of therapy, prayers, hopes, tears, couldn't fix us. I couldn't fix us. And he didn't seem to recognize the problem.

Our marriage had been over for a long time, but I continued to fight for it. I tried to make it healthy. I finally let go of the wish that he would fight for us, too. To fight meant to care. To care meant to make an investment. Bob had to fight for his sobriety every day. He invested in himself just to stay sober. Just to stay alive.

Long ago, I returned home after a visit with a grieving friend. We'd shared stories and exhausted our emotions to honor a memory. I was drained. I walked in my front door near dinnertime and was met by Bob with our toddler, Jillybean, perched on his hip. "What's for dinner?" he said. No "Hello." No "How'd it go?" No "How are they?" Just "What's for dinner?"

I swallowed my hurt and defensiveness. The attack had started earlier than expected, and when I had no answer, he thrust Jilly into my arms and stomped away. Near tears, I looked up and asked, "Lord, what am I going to feed my family tonight?" At that exact moment, the phone rang and my neighbor said, "Hi, Nancy! We ordered a pizza and they accidently delivered us two. Do you want it?" In the midst of my hurt, my question was answered. Tangibly. Immediately. And not with a cheap, frozen pizza, either. This one was delivered, hand tossed, piping hot with "the works." Manna from a pizza oven.

So I pursued God hard. I grew up in a church and loved Jesus, but still maintained a distance between my everyday life and my Sunday life. Now, I looked for mentors and began to meet people who did this God thing in a real way. A seven-days-a-week way. Who didn't wear Jesus masks of fake perfection on Sundays. Who let me see their struggles, failures, and humanness. Their honesty made me honest. I asked for prayer. I asked for guidance. I shared my pain and frustration and let them help, challenge, and grow me.

Bob did the best he could. So did I. But bit by bit, little by little, joy by joy, I disappeared. I was erased. I erased myself. I would let down my guard, let him back in, start to relax and get sucker punched by his words. Time and time and time again.

And then one day I asked myself, *What kind of role*

model am I? What does our damaged relationship teach our children about love and commitment? What do they see? What patterns will they repeat? Who will they become? Will they stay with someone, no matter what, because the image or fantasy is more important than the truth? Will they meekly accept whatever is dished out because their identity is wrapped up in what someone else thinks? Will they keep the peace at all costs because nothing (especially their true selves) is worth taking a stand for? Will they put everyone else's needs and comforts ahead of their own because everyone else is worth more than they are, especially if they earn more money? Will they treat their spouses like they're "Less Than" because they think they have the right to, based on nothing more than ego and earnings? Will they allow someone else to put them in a box and expect them to live within those limitations? Will they never have the courage to look within themselves, to take responsibility for their own actions? Will they always blame something or someone else for their circumstances? Is that what I want for them?

Marriage had been a means to an end for me. My clock was ticking. I wanted to be a mother. I had my mom's agenda and her timeframe. I heard the voice in my head—the voice I credited to her example—roar in my ears, "You're nothing without a man."

Timing is everything, and when I met Bob, I fell. Hard. I became a caricature of the '50s housewife, complete with the nice house and the cute kids—one girl and one boy. The king's family.

And yet it finally dawned on me that I hated who I was. I was NOT a caricature. I hated being married like this. And hated that I hated it. So I began to hate me.

5

Three weeks after Bob left, Winnie the Wonder Mutt adopted us. Reggie, still diligently on the case, suggested we install a security system, so Sam, Jill, and I headed to the Orphans of the Storm shelter and got one for $90. It was the best money I ever spent.

She put her paw out of her cage when Jill stopped in front of it. "Hey, Mom! What do you think of this one?"

I bent down to get a good look. "She's kind of a mishmash of parts," I said. "I think she's picked us." The three of us took her out to the exercise area, and I crouched in front of her, eye to eye.

"Do you want to come home and be our dog?" Her brown eyes locked with mine, and she licked me under my chin.

Thirty minutes later, Winnie sat her butt on the seat of the van with her paws on the floor, like she was semi-human and part of us all along. She was our missing link, now that we had a link to miss. Bob had never wanted a dog. Winnie was our celebration that Jill was home from the in-patient mental health program and was a warm, furry reminder that we would all be okay. With messy, wet dog kisses and furry snuggles, we began to heal.

We settled in and life fell into a manageable chaos. One morning after I took Sam to school, I walked into the empty house and stopped dead in my tracks. Something was different. No familiar knot in the gut. No eggshells to walk around. No Bob working in the basement, listening for my footsteps. I was alone. And I was at peace. In the midst of chaos. For the first time in—ever.

I jumped up onto the sill of the bay window.

"I hate these fucking blinds!" I yelled to no one. "I've always hated these fucking blinds!" So I took them down.

6

I took a lie detector test on November 12th.

"It's standard procedure when a spouse goes missing," Reggie assured me.

It wasn't like the movies where they strap your arm down and that machine with the little needle makes lines all over a graph. Just a lapel microphone that measures vocal stress. I was a little disappointed.

The officer who administered the test told me I would answer five simple questions. "However, when I ask you question number four—'What color is my briefcase?'—I want you to say brown instead of black, even though you see it's black."

Seriously, is this really happening? How'd I get here?

Brutally honest, my voice registered stress on the question **before** the one I was supposed to lie about because the thought of lying on the next one made me so stressed. So my name was cleared. The police no longer suspected that I knew where Bob was or had anything to do with his disappearance. I brought my mom with me for moral support and took her to brunch afterwards. Isn't that what you're supposed to do after you pass a lie detector test?

Later that afternoon, Reggie called to see if I could come to a press conference the next day. For some time, Bob's father and brother had pressed the sheriffs' department about why they didn't consider the case a homicide investigation. They were convinced there was "foul play." It had gotten very ugly. They knew I wanted a divorce. They knew that Keith was in the picture. I think they thought I had something to do with it. Instead, the police treated it as a missing person case. To defend his department, the sheriff called a press conference to justify their investigation.

"Reggie, I'll do it, but I don't think it's a good idea to have me anywhere near either of them. I WILL lose it." He withdrew his invitation.

To build their defense, the Sheriff's Department discovered a warrant for Bob's arrest. Would the surprises never end? Before we were married, he had gotten a driver's license using a false identity. One he'd purchased from God knows where. I was so blind and so in love that I let him use my car to take that driver's test. But then he got a DUI—and appeared in court as this other person. And then he failed to return for the continuance. I didn't know anything about that DUI. He had kept that a secret. And had I known, I would have ended the relationship back then. I may have been in love—or in love with the idea of being in love—but that kind of illegal behavior crossed a line I knew I wouldn't have crossed and knew I wouldn't have accepted.

This information was revealed during the press conference for all to see, so I had to have another difficult discussion with my children. My grief-stricken, bewildered children learned another life lesson that day. They found out that even though you may learn something the hard way and then change, the consequences don't go away. They follow you. The father they never saw drink anything other than a very occasional non-alcoholic beer had an alias AND a warrant for his arrest. My heart shattered. Again.

Two days later, my friend called at the crack of dawn. "Nancy, I just heard your name on the radio! They cleared you!"

"Wait! What? Okay." The sleep cobwebs left abruptly. "Well then, I'd better get up and shower so when the media shows up, I'm ready. They could be here any minute. Got to look good in case there are TV cameras, you know. Maybe Oprah will be here and she'll want me on her show!" What a crazy way to wake up. What a crazy life I was living.

A very public proclamation of innocence or … just another item checked off my "Crazy Shit That Actually Happened" list.

On to another "normal" week of surreal.

7

After the living room blinds came down, I started an avalanche of home improvement projects. Money was spent to do stuff around the house, and I kept a mental list in defense of what was done and why it mattered to ME. When Bob came back, I'd be ready.

If he came back.

As the days added up and the holidays loomed, we began to face "if."

With Winnie the Wonder Mutt in the back, we drove seven hours to southern Illinois for our "normal" extended family Thanksgiving. We stopped along the way to try to enjoy the trip, and when Winnie got her first hotel stay, she kept us distracted with her antics. A hard, awkward, weird, painful, vulnerable holiday. Grief and pain and blame were the not-so-secret ingredients in the stuffing.

Thanksgiving passed.

His birthday passed.

We survived.

We tried to create some new traditions for Christmas since old ones pointed out the void. Our new threesome stayed overnight in Chicago at a hotel with an indoor pool. We walked along Michigan Avenue, enjoyed the lights, and scanned the crowds for Bob's face as our brains tried to fill the empty space Bob had occupied.

The kids wanted a tree, but no one wanted to decorate one. Friends came over and hung the ornaments. A secret Santa left a basket of gifts for us. Sam got to "Shop with a Cop" through his counselor at school. Life was brittle and blurry and weird and nothing felt even remotely right.

We went to our "normal" Christmas Eve church service. Except nothing was "normal," and it felt worse to do the things that highlighted that. I cried through the whole service.

After church, the kids and I went to our friends' house for late night Christmas carols. Every year we'd been invited and every year Bob said no. So that year we said yes. And another new tradition came to life.

The question of "Is it best to maintain the same traditions for consistency or throw it all out and start over?" was ever present. The kids seemed to do better with experiences not associated with their dad. There were no memories to compare.

So Christmas passed and we all just held our breath and wanted to sleep until New Year's.

8

My pseudo-sister friend Laura saw me at Christmas and said, "Nan, you need to do a show." She was directing the musical *Urinetown* at the local community college, and I knew she was right. I hadn't performed in years. I had let the performer in me die. Now, I knew I needed to get reacquainted with that part of me, and I agreed to go to callbacks. Her direction and our relationship made it feel safe.

"I have the perfect part for you, and you will own it." Soupy Sue. Not too big or small a role. Just right.

I was a theatre major in college and had performed since the age of three. Grade school, high school, college, community, and professional theatre were where I felt at home. The stage was the place I became someone else for a few hours. The stage was the place I felt emotions that weren't acceptable in my real life. I acted, sang, and danced my heart open as my characters.

I found my identity in the identity of the role.

When I got married, theatre no longer fit my new life. Bob had a "wife" box for me to fit in, and I gladly climbed in and shut the lid. There was no room in the box for musicals. So Laura's offer that December was huge for me. It healed a fracture in my psyche.

My real story was too evolving, too heavy, too surreal, too *Movie of the Week*, so I kept it quiet. I needed to forget for a little while, set reality aside, feel distracted, and just be me. Nancy, just another cast member.

At times it felt hard and selfish, but I HAD to do that show, to put my needs first and trust it would be okay. To realize I couldn't fix the situation and, whether I did or didn't do *Urinetown*, Bob was still missing.

On rehearsal nights, Sam stayed home with all the lights on, TV volume up, Red Ryder BB gun pumped, and Winnie the Wonder Mutt at his side. Just in case his dad came back. One night he asked, "Mom, if Dad comes back, what should I do?"

"Well, Sam, you should call 911 because there are a lot of people who will want to ask him some questions, like where he's been. They've spent time looking for him and need to know he's found. Then, if I'm not here, you call me next, okay?" Our emergency plan. It hurt so much that Bob had become a monster, someone to be afraid of instead of a father welcomed home.

I channeled all I had into my performance as a washed up vaudevillian tap dancer. To feel the safety, escape, focus and fun of being Soupy Sue for a few hours each night at rehearsal was like a breath of cool, clean air. Refreshing. Comfortable. Instinctual. The part that didn't fit in Bob's "wife" box still fit me. It had been there all along.

Then the monkey mind set in: *Where the hell is he? He left us and that isn't a crime. What if he comes back? How do I move forward with the divorce after this stunt? He couldn't be dead. And he certainly couldn't have killed himself. Wouldn't do it. Nope. Not going there. What's he up to? Does he have a new life somewhere with a new identity? He's probably a caddy at some tropical country club incognito. Does he watch us twist in the wind from afar? He probably hopes that after all this we'll appreciate what he did for us. Does he think we won't dare take him for granted now? Where is he? Has he lost it? Will he hurt us? Is he okay?*

An infinity loop.

We were his mental captives, and I braced myself every time I opened the door to the garage. I expected to see his face. Expected to see the gun.

Every. Damn. Time.

I had dreams where he came back. I'd scream at him, pummel him with my fists. And then I'd wake up angry and exhausted. All the fears released in my sleep. How could he just leave us all hanging like this? Wondering. Seeing him everywhere on every corner.

My first thought every morning was, *Hmm. What should I wear if I have to go to the morgue today? Whatever I wear will be forever ruined as 'the outfit I wore when*

I identified Bob's body,' and I won't be able to wear it ever again. My second thought was to lean on Keith, who was still in Oregon, for support. It was all too hard by myself.

Where is this in the brochure? What are the instructions for proper morgue identification behavior? I braced myself for whatever came next and did my best to ride the wave of crazy.

Waiting.
Waiting.
Waiting.

9

Backstage for the first tech rehearsal, five days before *Urinetown* opened and five months *to the day* of Bob's disappearance, I got the call. Amy, my stalwart friend who had camped on our couch when Bob had first gone missing, showed up at the theatre—which was weird in and of itself—and told me that Reggie was looking for me. "Go be with her when I call. Make sure she isn't alone," he'd ordered. So she did as she was told. Surrounded by old theatre friends, the words "We believe we've found the place of your husband's demise," exploded through the phone and smashed full bore into my brain.

"We found the gun and his wedding ring." As I listened, numb, speechless, a part of me hovered above myself in a sort of out of body experience. I swear I detected a smirk in Reggie's voice as he said, "Of course, we'll have to do DNA testing on the bones for positive ID, because there's not much left."

"Not much left." There's not much left of my husband.

There's not much left of my children's father. There's not much left of Ginny's son. There's not much left of Tommy's brother. There's not much left of Robert Donald Nelson, human being. Reggie's words ricocheted through every cell of my body, and I just stood there, waiting for the ringing in my head to stop.

Then the performer in me kicked in, and my first thought was *The rehearsal must go on.* The call ended, and I processed—or rather didn't process—the weight of the news. *Well, there it is*, I thought, *and I'm still here. I'm a widow.* The irony of the place I was when I found out didn't escape me. Really? Are you kidding me? In the theatre?

I paced around for a few minutes. I tried to breathe. My mind raced. Laura left to explain the rehearsal delay to the cast. And then reality smacked me up side my head, and I knew I had to go home to tell my kids. The show must go on, but the rehearsal would have to go on without me.

I have no recollection of my phone conversation with Keith as I left the theatre. I picked up my mom on the way home so she would be with me when I showed up unannounced to make the biggest announcement of my kids' lives. I have no idea what we said on that ride. But I will never forget the faces of my beloved children at my unexpected arrival home with Grandma in tow: Jill, wrapped in a bath towel fresh from her shower and Sam, with Winnie snuggled close, looked at me with expectant, frightened eyes.

There really was no way to cushion the news. I took a deep breath and said, "They found your dad. He's dead. Looks like suicide. I am so sorry."

Moment frozen.

Forever.

10

After the difficult phone calls to family and friends, we hunkered down with the new reality. My show must go on and it did. With little left to identify Bob, I gave permission for DNA testing on the bones left behind. This would take a couple of weeks. We knew it was him. His wedding ring, watch, and the gun proved it. But we followed protocol. In the end, they found a tooth fragment, and our family dentist made the positive ID.

There was a certain guilty relief. Closure. We could stop seeing him everywhere we went or wondering if he'd ever come home again. He didn't scare us anymore. The threat was gone. Less than a mile from home.

The memorial service was set for a Friday afternoon in April. The 23rd. A day that worked in our schedule so that Jill could go on the college visit we'd planned for the week before. She desperately needed to focus on her future. Something hopeful after months of moving through each day on sheer guts and dread.

So we visited the aptly named Hope College in Holland, Michigan. In a phone conversation that will remain with me forever, I sat alone in our hotel room and called in Bob's obituary in order to make the deadline. Then, a couple of Bob's best friends who happened to live nearby took me to lunch, and we met Jill and her friend after their campus tour. As we all posed under the arch that marked the entrance to the college, I struggled to get a photo with all of us in the shot. At that moment, a girl and three guys skateboarded over to us.

As we posed with brave faces and tried to envision a future for fatherless Jill, the girl said, "Hey, would you like us to take your picture?" I thanked her and handed her the camera.

"I'm Daisy," she said. "Is there anything we can pray with you about?"

"Oh, here's where my mom cries," Jill answered.

We giggled, and I said, "Well, if you're serious, and you really want to know"—I didn't pause for a response—"her dad's funeral is next Friday. He was missing for five months before we got the news that he killed himself." Somehow, it was easier for me to refer to Bob as "her dad" instead of "my soon-to-be ex-husband if he'd lived."

Mouths gaped and the skateboarders' eyes grew deer-in-headlights huge. Daisy stammered, "We ... we were just praying in the pine grove when God told us to find the family under the arch by … by the yellow tulips." She gestured toward the flowerbed in full yellow bloom.

Tears welled up and rolled down my cheeks as I choked out, "Then, I guess we better do this!"

We all joined hands under the arch that said HOPE—Jill, her friend, her godfather (Bob's best friend), Daisy, and the three boys. Daisy prayed for us, and I prayed for them. I prayed Jeremiah 29:11, "For I know the plans I have for you, says the Lord. Plans to prosper you and not to harm you. To give you hope and a future." And how that verse sustained me. It reassured me that nothing was a surprise to God, and that He promises to turn our mourning into dancing.

We all hugged, and Daisy looked deep into my eyes. "You are the third person in two days to quote that scripture to me. I've struggled with why I'm here, why Hope College, why now? God knew I needed to meet the Nelsons."

She emailed a couple of days later to tell me that after we parted ways, mouths still agape, tears still wet on cheeks, she'd sat in front of the campus library when a friend walked by with a stroller. Daisy got up to speak to her and asked if she could pray for the baby.

The baby's name?

Jeremiah.

11

Methodists don't call it a funeral. At least some Methodists don't. At our church, we call it a Memorial Service. We choose to focus on the loved one's life and be positive about the impact and memories left behind. And so the Memorial Service for Robert Nelson was held on a Friday afternoon in April. But as I walked down that familiar aisle with my children, every step calculated and memorized, there were no right words.

What do you say?

Do I gloss over the empty space left behind? The tragedy. The loss. The pain. The broken pieces of a family trying to find a new true north. The complicated grief that coats our lives with a fine dust of guilt and regret.

What do you say?

Bob's relationship to me was as my "almost ex-husband who disappeared for five months—to the day—before we found out he'd killed himself." His relationship to his children was simply "Dad." After eighteen years of struggle (a.k.a. marriage), I'd finally found the courage to ask for a divorce. The reasons were deep and unique to us, as they are for anyone who has reached this conclusion. And the reasons were no one else's business. Yet, some of those "friends" who filled the pews that day thought they knew *our* story. *My* story. They acted as if they had the right to judge me. Sideways glances, stares, whispers and even blatant snubs to my face were part of that long walk down the aisle on one of the worst days in the life of my family.

What do you say?

As we sat in the front pew and listened to the eulogy Bob's brother gave, (interrupted several times by his mother) that was sprinkled with funny stories so that emotions could explode in an appropriate way, we were angry. Not the appropriate "Poor Me" anger at the unfairness of it all and the price of loss and sorrow. We were pissed off, flat-out angry that my "almost ex-husband who …" and their forever dad had left us. We were angry at the weirdness of it all, at the abstract fear and *unknowing* we'd lived through for the last five months. We were angry that he'd taken a gun and killed himself. We were angry that he would never be in that church as the father of the bride or groom. We were angry that his best friend, John, had walked in our door that morning with a shoe, sock still inside, a scrap of plaid, and a single sunglass lens. "I can't believe they left this there. He was a person!" He had gone to the "scene of the crime" and returned with artifacts of his friend. Artifacts of an almost ex-husband and forever father.

We were pissed off angry that we were pissed off angry. Period.

What do you say?

The pews were packed with bodies, each one somehow braided with Bob. Bodies that had been connected to both of us, our couple friends, floated around on the edges. Divorce is its own hardness. But this? This permanent absence reality was bigger. Way bigger. Brave bodies came through the line to hug and stand in the awkwardness with me. Other bodies picked the other line. The line of his family. The line to watch the video of his life that didn't include one single photo of me. After eighteen years of marriage. Not one single photo.

The usual condolences didn't fit. Yes, I'd wanted a divorce. But I hadn't wanted a death. And certainly not a suicide.

In terms of closure for the five-month odyssey we'd traveled together, the memorial service was anti-climactic. A necessary and respectful conclusion for a life that ended too soon in an unimaginable way. We were surrounded by bodies that were hungry for words of comfort and assurance from us that we would be okay. And by *we*, I really meant *ALL* of us. The saga had an end now, and we all had permission to move on. To move through the stages of grief past disbelief. It was real and tragic and over.

For my children and me, it was just the beginning of a forever trek along the uneven path of anger, grieving, and healing. Of moving on. One life was over. Many more lives were rerouted through uncharted territory. A path that never ends and that would wind through our lives forever, just as Robert Nelson was part of us then and now and always.

What do you say?

12

Once, when I sat on a coroner's jury, we had to determine the cause for every death that had happened that wasn't in a hospital or nursing home. Was it from natural causes, homicide, an accident, or suicide? With suicide, the grief is much angrier and the pain goes much deeper. It's complicated. The questions don't end, and the closure has temporary moments. The brain space and presence that Bob now took up in our family was greater in death than in life.

We all struggled to understand how he could do *it*, why he did *it*, what if he hadn't done *it*, what life will be like now that he has done *it* … the list goes on. We braided the *it* into our lives, so we could cope and eventually thrive, even though we realized that the *it* came from somewhere and not out of nowhere.

I admit it. I am guilty of downplaying the permanence and seriousness of mental illness. Doesn't "illness" conjure the image of a period of sickness followed by wellness or cure? For people living with mental illness, there is no cure or magic solution to remove it, to make it just go *poof* and disappear. Yet we often tell those who suffer to snap out of it! It's just a phase. You'll get over it. Or the one I'm particularly guilty of: "Focus on the good things in your life and just do something, anything other than just lie there. I know you'll *feel* better."

Like the old "Take two aspirin and call me in the morning" tactic. Shame on me.

Mental illnesses are very common; in fact, they are more common than cancer, diabetes, or heart disease. According to the National Alliance of Mental Illness (NAMI):

> Approximately 43.8 million adults in the U.S. or 18.5 percent experience mental illness in a given year. Even though mental disorders are widespread in the population, the main burden of illness is concentrated in a much smaller proportion. There are about 1 in 25 Americans, who suffer from a serious mental illness (one that significantly interferes with functioning). It is estimated that mental illness affects 1 in 5 individuals in America.

Yet we still call it mental *illness*.

Also according to NAMI:

> Approximately 60 percent of adults, and almost one-half of youth ages 8 to 15 with a mental illness received no mental health services in the previous year.

Suicide is the tenth leading cause of death in the U.S. (more common than homicide) and the third leading cause of death for ages 15 to 24 years. More than **90 percent** of those who die by suicide had one or more mental disorders.

Those statistics are staggering. Yet they are just numbers.

When you love someone who took their life, those statistics become flesh and blood. But because we focus on how their life ended, it becomes their whole story. We spend countless hours trying to figure out what they were thinking when they did *it*. We try to wrap our unaffected minds around the end, rather than realizing that their illness won. We might not have even known they were suffering, undiagnosed and unsupported. We call them selfish or impulsive or cowardly. Or, we survivors suffer in silence. This grief is complicated. Unlike other deaths where loved ones and friends share stories of the lost one, no one wants to talk about the death-by-suicide person. Very few subjects make people as uncomfortable as suicide. Shame on us.

Why the stigma?

The very definition of the word *stigma* means disapproval or dishonor. Synonyms for stigma include: taint, blot, black mark, stain, blemish, disgrace. So why do we feel this very real stigma around the subjects of mental illness and suicide?

Bob died by his own hands. I would say he killed himself except it wasn't really him. Saying he killed himself gives the impression that it was a choice he made when his death was actually the end result of mental *illness*. But isn't that the way most of us feel? That somehow there was a rational pro/con list that resulted in their choice to end their life?

So we ponder in solitary silence. And we don't talk about it. Why?

Is it because of fear? Because all of us, if we're being completely honest, have thought for a fleeting moment in deep despair that it might be better if we weren't here. Admit it. We've all had the thought that death might be better than the pain we felt in that moment. Let's stop pretending we have it all together all the time. We don't. Suicide hits close to home. It's relatable. And that scares us.

Is it because of guilt? We agonize about the role we played. Should we have known what was going on and been able to stop them? Could we have helped them make another, different *choice*? Did we miss something? Were we so self-absorbed that someone we love suffered right in front of our faces, but we couldn't see past ourselves? We failed to take control of the (uncontrollable) situation when we *should* have and missed the signs, so we feel horribly, horribly guilty.

We can sympathize with those who have lost their battle with cancer or a physical disease, but we have a difficult time with those who lost their battle with mental illness. Suicide isn't, in our minds, the heroic end of a battle with physical disease like cancer, where every treatment was tried but ultimately couldn't keep the disease at bay. But for many people with mental illness, they have fought for years through countless treatments. But it's different somehow. "*Mental* illness isn't supposed to be terminal!" our rational minds cry. It's not like our cells have run amok and are on a rampage to destroy our organs. Mental illness is just all in the mind. But, the statistics tell a different story. More than 90 percent of those who die by suicide had one or more mental disorders, and yet we have a misguided notion that when mental illness is terminal, it was the result of a *choice*. Would we ever think someone who died of cancer *chose* to die of cancer?

So the stigma of mental illness and suicide continues as our limited brains try to fathom the choice. But it wasn't a *choice*, and those of us left behind can't fathom that, so we stay silent.

13

Being the financial head of my household is one of the hardest things I've done. "You're nothing without a man ..." blared like a siren in my head. *I can't do this! What am I thinking?* The terror of our monthly bills loomed at the edge of my consciousness. What's due and when? Bob had always handled every aspect of our financial life. Family finances weren't my job. I was out of my comfort zone.

When Bob left, I went through our expenses and canceled everything that wasn't absolutely necessary. This seemed like a fitting response to his absence. It was what I *should* do, right? But how do you deal with, "Ma'am, we have to speak to the account holder, Robert Nelson, in order to cancel your cable service"? Shooting back, "Well, I need to speak to Robert Nelson, too, so if you find him, ask him to give his wife a call, will you? He disappeared October 7th without a trace," was strangely satisfying and usually effective.

I developed budgets. I blew budgets. I tried to wrap my

brain around cash flow while feeling stupid and small and immature and unprepared. I juggled the needs of two devastated children and a full-time job of grief containment while I worked at my church and kept the house running.

I said *yes* to things I never would have before because I was too tired and worn down to say *no*. I said *yes* because Bob almost always said *no*. I said *yes* in the hope that it might ease the kids' pain, in the hope it would make the house feel like mine, that it would offer some dim, short-lived glimmer of happiness, that *yes* would fix the mess.

I said *yes* because it made me feel safe and because *no* made me feel guilty.

"*Please forgive me.*" We got a dog.

"*Please forgive me.*" We got an Xbox.

"*Please forgive me.*" We're going to Florida.

Even though I knew in my gut that Bob died by his own hand, there wasn't conclusive proof. Five months to the day had passed, with little "evidence" to know exactly what happened. According to the Forest Preserve guy that our local paper quoted, "The bones had been gnawed on by animals," which is what every mother dreams her children will read about their dad.

I ripped that guy a new one.

"Look, I know this was pretty exciting stuff compared to the rabid skunk or whatever you usually deal with in your job. And, hey, I know you didn't know those bones were my husband's, but you DID know they were human.

You DID know they belonged to a person in a family. So the next time, God forbid, you discover human remains, please watch what you say to the press. My kids read YOUR words that their dad was 'gnawed on by animals.' They've suffered enough, and you added to it. It was entirely insensitive."

"I'm sorry for your loss," he said and hung up on me.

Asshole.

Because there wasn't "enough left" to prove Bob had committed suicide, when the life insurance guy called and asked for the cause of death, I could say "Undetermined." It felt safe, even though the suicide clause of Bob's life insurance had long expired. I didn't want any questions, investigations, or excuses to not pay out what Bob had so faithfully paid in for years to protect us. I was so damn tired of questions and assumptions and sick of spending so much brain space and energy on all of it.

At the social security office, death certificate in hand, I let the grateful tears fall. With the survivor benefits, we could make ends meet. We could do this. We would make it. I could keep my part-time job at the church, my safe harbor during this tsunami. Predictable and solid when all else was so fragile and brittle and raw and weird and different and wobbly.

I seesawed between selling our home and staying, but the thought of moving clutched at my stomach and hammered at my head. How could we pack, paint, fix, or toss accumulated stuff we weren't ready to let go of yet? How could we list and show the house, find somewhere new, apply for a mortgage and, the biggie, what if I found out *I* wasn't enough, didn't make enough, didn't have enough?

So we stayed, and the first major adult financial decision made? I paid off the mortgage on the house. I'm a big girl now. A 100 percent homeowner.

We'll just deal with the ghosts the best we can, I rationalized. *Maybe, over time, we'll find it comforting to be here.* Our whole world was different already, so we needed some same.

"They" advise anyone who has suffered a close death to not make any major decisions the first year. What they don't tell you is that *every* decision feels major. ***Every*** decision saps your energy. ***Every*** decision feels heavy and important. Trust your gut and do what feels best for you. And accept that it is really fucking hard. And that's okay.

It took so much energy to contain my children's grief. It took so much energy to figure out the household finances. It took so much energy to do my job well. It took so much energy to invest in my relationship with Keith. It took so much energy to grieve.

In the middle of it all, I began to see how Bob had provided for us. He paid extra principle on the mortgage. He paid bills on time every month for all those years. And I began to understand what "love" meant to him. To Bob, love meant being the Provider and Doer of all the "right" things. That he could take care of his family financially made him feel like he had life under control. That word again—control.

Our first Christmas as parents, Bob was in his first year of business. His father had fired him the December before. Money was tight. I was at home taking care of a baby. He was at home building a business. There were times we couldn't afford diapers. My parents would buy them for us and bring them over for their granddaughter.

My brother gave us a gift certificate to a local grocery store. I was so touched. Bob was so pissed. I felt loved. Bob felt judged.

"Your brother doesn't think I can take care of my family," he hissed.

How could I explain to him that my family was different? We were connected by a rope of love, not a bungee cord of obligation. My family's intentions were pure. This was just what we did for each other.

His reaction was a huge indicator that his self-worth was tied to his earning potential. His sense of success relied on his bank balance, his salary. I finally understood this about him. For years, I reassured him that he was far more to me, to our family, than just a paycheck.

This way of life was okay at first. It felt familiar and it worked. I watched my Mom stay home with us, and I watched Dad march off to work every day. There was a part of me that really liked our traditional arrangement. I felt cared for and safe. Then I began to feel guarded and alone.

On Friday, March 5th, 2010, I sat in the bank parking lot and bawled. I was close to broke and angry at myself because I hadn't realized the breadth and depth of the chaos. I hadn't budgeted well. I hadn't been scared enough. I felt like I was nothing without Bob. I was ignorant, and I was frustrated that time had passed with no closure, no word, no resolution, no relief. I was angry because the bank wouldn't cash out a CD in Bob's name, even though I was the beneficiary. They didn't care about my reality. Rules were rules.

"We're terribly sorry, but with no death certificate, the money is still his, whether he's missing or not." Their pity poured out along with their words.

I broke down and thought, *I'm that woman! The one who has nothing and nowhere to turn. I'm pathetic. How much longer can I do this? I can't do this. I'm so fucking tired!* My lawyer had started the process of the divorce, so we could divide our assets under these extenuating circumstances. "In the meantime," he urged me, "borrow some money to tide you over."

So I did what any good daughter would do. I called my mom and bawled out the details.

Two days later I got the call that Bob was dead.

14

As life started to settle down, I began to appreciate Bob more, and I began to truly grieve.

I couldn't fix this. From the moment he left, it was way too big. I'd worked hard my whole married-and-mother life to make everything okay for our family. But this? I was powerless to make it better. Wasn't the definition of a good mom one who kept her children safe, who worked to make their life easier, to make it shiny and wonderful and magical? I had to figure out a new way.

I learned to sit with them in their grief and pain, even though I knew there was no easy solution. I had to give them the space and permission to try to make sense of something senseless, and to design their new reality—one without a dad and one with a mom who was now very different from the one they had grown up with.

It wasn't my fault.

I felt selfish. I feel selfish. I pray that someday my children will understand that I couldn't stay that same mom.

That they will remember me as the mom who kept getting up, no matter how many times life knocked her down. That I did the best I could and never, ever meant to hurt them.

It wasn't my fault.

Guilt keeps me small. I tell myself over and over it was because Bob lost his battle with mental illness that he did this, not because of me. Most days I believe this, and I am in awe of how far we've come and all we've learned. Some days I go backward to those first days, to the oppressive guilt. But we continue on, this new family. We are all real now, and every day we learn to love all the parts of ourselves in our new realness. It's messy and hard, even this many years later. But it's also powerful and beautiful and honest.

It wasn't my fault.

As we struggled with this evolution, I questioned what the "normal" bumps of teenage/young-adult years were and what bumps were created by Bob's suicide. It all blurred together, and I couldn't fix it. I still can't fix it. At times, I feel powerless. Guilt ruled me for so many years and kept me from asking anything of my kids, which made it so much harder to ask them later. Clean their rooms? Do chores? After all they've been through? What if they hate me? What if my request becomes the straw that breaks the camel's back, and they kill themselves? But I'm learning that it's okay and safe to ask, and even require, that they help me.

It wasn't my fault.

Our job as good parents is to become jobless, to be downsized by our children. If we do our job well, they become worthwhile, productive adults who don't need us to tie their shoes or kiss every "boo boo." If we don't do our job well, they'll never grow up. They'll stay small and dependent and won't spread their wings and find their own mission in life. But parenting is hard and sometimes we have to be a hard-ass. Parenting is not a popularity contest because there is no contest at all. No one wins and yet everyone does—eventually.

It wasn't my fault.

Children sputter and fight and cry and scream and push every button they can find to stay in their little protected world. They lash out and hit us in our Achilles's heel: guilt. But it isn't our fault. The more we repeat this, we eventually believe it, and it becomes our truth.

It isn't our fault.

As I reach this new place of "never been before," what keeps me sane is to stay present in this exact moment, so I don't get pulled into the ugly terrain of guilt land. I know in my gut that I am doing the best I can. Each and every day I work on forgiveness toward Bob, myself, toward everyone. And I grieve.

It wasn't my fault.

My tribe of high school friends keeps me grounded with their understanding, advice, and permission to be real, scared, frustrated, and tired. I need their support, strength, and love. They know they don't have to fix things for me, but they can just sit with me and understand how hard and relentless my life can be as I grapple with a son who struggles to understand what it means to be a man with no father to guide him and a daughter who grieves the loss of the dad she adored. It's like learning how to go through life missing a limb or one of your senses. You can do the same things everyone does, but the extra effort takes more stamina, creativity, and guts that you sometimes just don't have. So it takes longer or looks different.

It wasn't my fault.

But we do the best we can and we are still here ...

And that *IS* my fault. In a good way.

15

The second year is harder than the first. Sorry. I wish I could be the good news fairy and tell you that if you "gut out" the first year, it's all easy as pie after that. Nope.

The first year is just odd and off and strange and blurry and stabbing and numb. The second year brings focus to the fact that life is forever changed. This is just how it is now. It doesn't end. Bob won't come back. Ever. Holidays, celebrations, anniversaries, and birthdays will never be the same.

Elizabeth Kubler-Ross, Swiss psychiatrist and author, said, "The reality is that you will grieve forever. You will not 'get over' the loss of a loved one; you will learn to live with it. You will heal and you will rebuild yourself around the loss you have suffered. You will be whole again, but you will never be the same. Nor should you be the same, nor would you want to."

The Next Right Thing—A Journal Entry
October 2011

The first year was like fog. Every now and then there would be a shift in the mist and some semblance of something familiar would appear for just long enough to give me my bearings. For a moment. I'm sure we ate, slept, and continued to breathe. We even managed to share a laugh or two, get our beloved dog, visit family in awkward holiday settings, and learn. I managed to hold down my job, play soccer, work on my long distance relationship with Keith, and try to be a mom. But mostly, I was terrified. All the time. At the beginning, before we knew the brutal truth, it was: Will he come back? What if he comes back? What if he doesn't? Will my children heal from this? Will they blame me?

Who was I kidding? Of course, they blamed me. The real question was and is: Will they ever forgive me?

After Bob's body was discovered, the "whys" set in. Why did he do it? Why didn't I see the signs? Why couldn't he have connected with me, which would have made all the other events unnecessary? Why couldn't he get help? Why was he so afraid?

Why? Why? Why?

Now, it's two years later. Why isn't it better? I

guess, in many ways, it is better. We're moving forward. Slowly, but surely. But now I cry. A lot. More than in the past. Almost as if, as reality sets in, I am thawing out. I grieve, but not for the life I had or even for him. I grieve for the predictability I knew. I grieve for what my kids are going through. For a loss so big there aren't enough syllables to describe it. I grieve for my humanness, that even though I used to fix everything—or fooled myself into thinking I could fix everything—I cannot fix this. I grieve for the energy I used to have. Grief is hard work. I am tired.

Tired. Tired. Tired.

And yet, I am blessed. God's timing is so very mysterious. My son is moving forward and is ready to embrace high school in a huge bear hug. Of course, he hasn't started yet and only has his sister's experience for comparison. And her experience was cut short on October 7th of her junior year when her father disappeared and life as she knew it ended. Actually, that's a lie. It ended July 28th when I asked her dad for a divorce. When I began my quest to become healthy. Living a healthy life remains my quest, and the rest of the crew will be dragged along for the ride in hopes they will get healthy, too.

Recovering from a recovering alcoholic is never easy. Recovering from the repercussions of suicide is never easy. The unbraiding process is hard, complicated, and incestuously embedded in our very DNA. Layers upon layers.

Layers. Layers. Layers.

I wonder whether or not this life will ever feel normal. Familiar. Sometimes I get lost in the freedom to roam around myself. To discover or rather rediscover so many parts of myself I'd let die. Hopes, needs, goals. I rein myself in and then remember I am free to explore now. But what about the parts of myself that have been long neglected, that like an untended yard, have grown weed infested? I avoid them unless I'm alone. Then I cry. I try to understand and forgive, but I fail more than I succeed. The brambles are oh so thick and the thorns are oh so sharp when I thought sure they would be worn down and less painful from the time passed and the storms weathered. My push through the undergrowth of my life has left me wounded, tender, scarred. Oh, so many scars.

Scars. Scars. Scars.

Today my thought was that I hoped Bob hadn't suffered. I drove by the park where he did it, like I have a million times before, and that was my thought. It knocked the wind out of me. I also had the tiniest stirring to find the spot. In all this time, I have not had the slightest urge to see what he saw last. Today I did. And I have no idea why. It's all still so new, so final, and yet I can't imagine my life any way other than it is right now. Today. If we'd gotten divorced, I can't imagine weekends without my kids while they stayed with him. I can't imagine what kind of psychological hold he would still have on me if the break hadn't been so abrupt and permanent. I don't like that he took control out of God's hands, and I hate that he robbed my kids of the opportunity to see him grow and mature as a human being. And I despise that he has cast a pall over every significant date that will ever exist in my children's lives. Because of him, nothing will ever be as truly joyful as it was meant to be. The anticipation of these events sucks the already compromised joy out even more. That's the part I will never fully forgive. I can only surmise and assume and give benefit of the doubt that he was in so much pain that all the ramifications far and wide of his incredibly selfish act didn't enter into even a corner of his psyche. I really thought he would finally deal with his demons. Silence the voice from his past that said he wasn't good enough. Make peace with his past. Grow to become the best Bob he could be. Leaving him was the wakeup call I couldn't get across any other way, but it seems the demons won.

Forever. Forever. Forever.

What do I do with this elephant in every room, this burden I carry with me wherever I go? Stigma. Pity. Curiosity. Like I'm a traveling exhibit at a museum from the city of "Don't Go There." It's strange that when I finally stopped living my life for everyone else and began to take care of myself, everyone else's interest level in me suddenly peaked. "How are you doing with all this?" "Why did it happen?" "What's your secret to handling it all?" Reminders that no one really cares about anyone else's story except for what they "get" from it. It might be as simple as advice or as complicated as a sense of belonging, one sufferer to another. I don't think this sideshow gawking is purposeful. I just think no one truly has that level of empathy. If we did, we would spend our lives in intense psychic pain from all the suffering in the world.

Heavy. Heavy. Heavy.

I'm reading *The Other Side of Sadness* by George A. Bonanno for my Perspectives in Prior Learning class at National Louis University. I have to write a seven- to fifteen-page paper about my experience with death and dying for college credit. It is important to finish the degree I started in 1981. FOR ME. Bonanno's book considers grief as something we are intrinsically wired to experience because loss is a natural and unavoidable human experience. It looks at what makes people resilient in the face of tragedy and loss. I like the idea that I'm somehow resilient. But why am I resilient and other people aren't? Is it just a matter of fact? That I had to go forward, go to work, continue on even though others can't?

Why? Why? Why?

Every relationship is braided together with experiences that create memories. The process of unbraiding the living person and rebraiding the memories is lifelong and exhausting and bittersweet. Laughter follows tears that follow laughter and still more tears. Life goes on. Grief never ends and that is okay. Grief becomes attached to memory and it's a placeholder for the important person we've lost. Death is part of life and goodbyes are hard. They're supposed to be. That exit mattered.

Why don't we talk about grief? It is a normal part of our human experience, and we experience loss in numerous ways all our lives, not just physical death. Every transition in life is loss. Marriage is loss of singlehood. Divorce is loss of marriage. Sickness is loss of health. Unemployment is loss of work. Relocation is the loss of place. Growth is even loss of our former familiar place of being. We don't want to call it grief. But it is. And grief doesn't have to be sad all the time. If we respect its power and what it represents, it becomes our new way of being, and because of the lifelong-ness of it, we will experience joy, laughter, anger, and peace in the midst of grief.

Grief is a doorway to a new start, the "before" and "after" of loss. We don't choose the loss most of the time, but even if we did, there is still change and grief. We're made to live in connection with people. People die. Circumstances change. We are wired to handle loss. Grief is personal and intimate. There isn't a "right" or "wrong" way to grieve. However, here is a nugget to help deal:

Be honest about your struggle! You don't have extra energy to waste by creating the "I've got my shit together" facade, so stop!!

Right now! I mean it!

Use your energy to love and be gentle with yourself. Treat yourself with the same loving kindness and compassion you would offer a grieving friend. Keep breathing. Deep belly breaths to help you remember you're not drowning. It only feels that way sometimes.

Nobody can change what happened.

I wish Bob hadn't died. I wish he could have gotten help, but he didn't. And that cannot be changed. His death is part of our lives now, and that truth slowly weaves its way into our reality. So do the memories. And in our grief, we are more real and true and honest than ever before.

There are days when my anger and frustration at the powerlessness to fix this get the best of me. When getting out of bed in my usual sparkly way is just not going to happen. When grief slaps me hard upside the head and saps my energy. I still mentally beat myself to a pulp for being weak and vulnerable. And human. Welcome to "My Day, Week, or Month of Self Hatred."

But as time passes, those days are different and more rare. I can deal with them and even welcome them *sometimes* because I know they usually come right before a period of huge personal growth. They don't scare me like they used to. They don't last as long, either. I try really hard to not judge myself. I take deep breaths, and those moments pass.

The ability to turn that attitude corner has transformed my inevitable grief days into gifts. Those days slow me down and let me knit myself back together in all my beautiful, imperfect perfection. I practice gentleness and self-care. Notice I said "practice," because sometimes I don't get it very right. I'm still learning. Sometimes I still beat the shit out of myself, but I'm getting worse at that and better at being loving. I focus on my blessings and slow down. I've been in this place enough times to know it won't kill me, that it doesn't last long and amps up the contrast in my life. The down days make the up days more vivid in every way. I don't want "beige."

That's the stuff that makes all of us interesting and amazing and unique. That's the stuff that brings our realness to light and makes us passionate, connected, and emotional humans. That's the stuff that sticks and becomes our sacred us.

16

Bob and I started marriage counseling when Jillian was eighteen months old. Becoming parents had compounded our struggles. The smooth moments were the exception in our relationship, and I hoped that talking to someone might make them the rule.

As I look back, I realize every significant moment of our marriage is tainted by some memory of anger. Translation? I felt hurt most of the time. But I wouldn't admit how hurt I was because that meant sadness and revealed my weak spot. Honesty made me vulnerable. Anger became my armor. That anger boiled below the surface, and its heat distracted me from the real issues.

Melissa was our counselor, and her first words to us were, "Congratulations on making it through sobriety. Most couples don't." We saw her for about six months as a couple before I let Bob off the hook and went alone. I would do my part, but Bob would not. I now know that he couldn't. But back then, I felt he didn't care enough, that this was all some big joke. That he thought I'd get over whatever my silly female need was. That our marriage, family, and *I* weren't worth the effort. My anger grew because my hurt grew. The day I told him to not bother going with me anymore made him so happy. The confirmation that HE was fine (even though deep down, he most certainly was not fine at all), and I was crazy. When I continued to go alone, it was confirmation that I was the one who needed help.

I worked with Melissa for almost ten years. There was a lot of work to do on a lot of issues. Rain or shine, week in, week out, I went. I wanted to stop living a life of reaction and figure out the puzzle pieces of me. She "re-mothered" me by accepting my differences, my uniqueness. Things that weren't what my mom was or thought her daughter should be. Melissa helped me find my place in the world, separate from my mom. She taught me to be myself, even when it felt like that rocked the fragile balance with others. Especially with my mom. The work that most daughters do as teenagers was the work of my thirties.

This process was horrendously hard at times. It felt disloyal and traitorous and endless. My mother-daughter enmeshment was so deep and so set, but I began to figure *me* out. Confidence grew from the permission to be authentic and brave. And me.

Little by little I changed, and so did every other relationship in my life. Melissa helped me understand that you can't change anyone else—only yourself and the way you choose to react. When you change, others either do, too, or they leave. Some left.

Several years after my last visit, I sent her an email:

> Hey Melissa! I just wanted to tell you how much I appreciate all the work you did with me. Your impact on our family has been tremendous. I have been Coordinator of Junior High Ministries at my home church for six months now and have put so, so much of what you taught me into practice. I work with adolescents on a daily basis (as well as having one of my own: Jill is almost fifteen and is a freshman!) and see so much of their struggle. I am proud to say I remember much of my own, which allows me to have great compassion and understanding. I feel blessed to be here.
>
> Sam is in fourth grade now and is an amazing young man already. He plays hockey, soccer and has such a kind heart. Everyone loves Sam. Jill is a leader in every way and is navigating life so much better than I did at her age. She has incredible gut instinct, insight, and rarely doubts herself. Pretty cool, huh?
>
> Bob and I have been married for seventeen years now. We have finally reached equilibrium and my working part-time has helped. About four years

ago, he finally confessed that he had binged on those weekends up north, which explained so many of the behavior patterns around those trips. (And confirmed that I Wasn't Crazy!!) By Bob finally "coming clean," he was able to be the man I always hoped he'd be during the difficult time of losing my dad (2/28/04). It was an incredible death with all of us there. My dad called the shots all the way to the very end. My mom has flourished and grown.

You've been on my heart lately, and I really felt the need to connect and thank you. If you ever have one of those days when you wonder if you're making a difference, know you made a huge one and continue to as we all do this thing called life.

Love, Nancy

Her response:

Nancy, I can't tell you how wonderful it was to hear from you. Your timing was perfect. It was one of those times I was questioning what I was doing in the field, my competency, impact, etc. My, how Spirit works in unexplainable ways ... I am so happy to hear that you have put your awesome spiritual and theatrical energy to use! Passionate, dedicated, intelligent, articulate, feeling. I can't think of a better fit for your interests and skills.

Your kids are fortunate to have a mother full of compassion, forgiveness and love. The fact that Jill has gut instinct, insight, rarely doubts herself, and is a leader, is a direct result of your parenting. She is so blessed to have a mom who was and is willing to take responsibility for her thoughts and feelings, a mom who validates her daughter, a mom who truly sees her daughter. I can't believe Sam is in the fourth grade.

What a wonderful model of relationship for your friends, community, and most importantly your kids. No relationship is a breeze. Nothing gets good and just stays that way. Life is about loving others and ourselves through the ups and downs. So easily said, so much harder—nearly impossible to practice. I was blown away by what you shared about Bob's confession. I think you intuitively knew it because of comments you'd make to me at the time. How validating to know that what you were feeling and the patterns were real—that there was a real cause for them!

Nancy, the work you are doing is moving. Working with the spiritual lives of children, helping them to discover, embrace, and operationalize the most powerful idea that we are spiritual beings with the ability and power to impact one another and the world in huge ways can be for you a tremendous reward and a huge responsibility. Your work will change our world for the better. Wow!

I loved hearing from you. I have so much gratitude for your thoughts.

Melissa

Shortly after Bob disappeared, I reached out to her again. "Google Bob Nelson." She immediately replied "Oh my God, Nancy. When do you want to come in?!" Her office became the only place it felt okay for me to curl into fetal position and just cry. The only place I could take off my superhero cape and just rest.

She was the first person to hug me after Bob's memorial service and to whisper, "I'm sending you love and light." Melissa knew how hard that day was. The pain, anger, sadness, snubs, looks of accusation. Bearing so much grief weight for my children.

She unconditionally supported and loved me through the thick and the thin, the think and the feel of it all. She let me lean on her until I grew strong enough to stand on my own.

17

Things have happened in my life that are so specific, so personal, and so intimate that I just can't call it chance or coincidence. I call it Godcidence. Still, God was in a box for me. A big box, custom made, but a box nonetheless.

Bob's disappearance blew the box apart. God was next to me, and I wrestled with him. Daily. Hourly. He was my three-legged race partner, joined together at the ankle, arms around each other. I went through this messiness in the fishbowl of being on church staff. People watched me. Watched my family. They examined us closely, and I hope they saw real.

God gave me courage to be honest. Permission to hurt and not put on a brave, fake mask. Many in my church family grieved with us. They loved Bob, too. They did not sit in judgment when the end came. And God grew bigger and became box busting for us all. In fact, my eighth grade confirmation class got front row seats to the shit show of my life that year.

My relationship with God isn't at all about "The Church" part of faith. It's living it out 24/7. Outside the Christian bubble of fake. I know too many people who are pillars by day, but juryless judges by night. Hypocrites. If you want to do faith the easy way, stick to what you know. Hang out with people who you like and are like you and who reinforce your facade. Send your money to good causes, do an occasional mission trip to those "less fortunate," and serve them. It will make you feel good, help someone somewhere, and looks nice on your life resume.

But if you think Christianity is easy, you're doing it wrong.

"Love One Another As I Have Loved You." There it is. The whole point. Why we're here. To lay it on the ultimate line for someone who, God forbid, might have a different lifestyle or background or belief system.

I follow the Jesus who met the woman at the well. She was there in the afternoon because all the gossipy, cliquey village people had made life so uncomfortable for her that she couldn't hang out with them at the usual time they all got their water. She had a "reputation," if you know what I mean. Her village sat in judgment of her and made her an outcast. Maybe they knew her circumstances. Her story. But I doubt it. And whether they did or didn't doesn't matter. They judged her. And instead of doing the hard work of giving her a love lifejacket in her stormy sea of life, they pushed her out of the community dinghy. Excluded her. Made and kept her small.

Not Jesus. He broke cultural norms and talked to her. Treated her with respect. Back then, they were enemies from different cultures. And to top it off, she had a bad rep. Jesus told her HER story, and it blew her mind. He didn't shame her with her mistakes. He didn't say he'd only love her and be her Savior once she got her act together. In that moment, He saw her. He heard her. And He understood her. And THAT transformed her.

She went back to judgment village with the news that she had just seen God, the Messiah who knew everything about her. You can bet those judgers looked at her through a different lens after that. Or maybe she didn't care about what other people thought anymore because she had been in the presence of the Almighty, and He made her feel whole. She didn't need anyone else's approval or validation because Jesus loved her *real*.

And every one of us is that woman. And Jesus loves our *real*.

That's why God sent him. To flesh out deity. Nothing pisses me off like judgmental, hypercritical, barrier-building believers. Love wins. Every time. Every single solitary human being has value and purpose and has God's thumbprint on their heart. We are all meant for big things. But those big things don't necessarily mean fame and fortune. Our big thing may be to teach our children how to buck the culture. Our big thing may be to encourage people to love and care for themselves, so they can overflow to others. Our big thing might be to save a life by noticing the pain.

The longer I live, the more I see our connections and sameness. And there's room for so much more. We are all created by the same designer who made everything. And we are brilliant designs. This realization of connection grows my idea of who/what God is and blows him out of any box my humanity tries to construct. It also has me in a pretty constant state of awe at the complexity of people. And that's a pretty cool way to live.

Maybe it's a cultural thing or religious relic, but our constant, self-inflicted beat down has to grieve God. Sure, we all make mistakes and fall short of what we could have done, but it seems we get stuck examining ourselves under the microscope of failure. Then, because we feel bad about ourselves, we turn outward and look for other people's "bad" to make us look and feel better by comparison. We feel small, so we want other people to feel small, too.

Misery loves company. If we're all miserable together, we don't know how miserable we actually are. It's only when someone comes along who embodies contentment and real and love that we realize how unhappy, fake, and lonely we are. We see how we're actually actively making choices to focus on the "less than."

We can beat ourselves up for choices we made in our un-do-overable past and stay stuck. Many do. OR we can give ourselves grace and forgiveness and love. If we do the "OR," we can give others grace and forgiveness and love, too.

"Love your neighbor as yourself ..." Mark 12:31. Which means love yourself.

First.

18

Relationships are not permanent. A reason, a season, a lifetime ... and lifetime relationships are rare, indeed. Things end. Relationships end because circumstances change. Someone moves away or has a life stage shift. They go back to work or get more involved in something that takes more of their time. There's a rift or an argument. Things become awkward. Sometimes they just fade away. Sometimes someone dies.

Those who jumped my USS *Relation "ship"* were uncomfortable with my new *REAL*. I moved out of my unhealthy marriage and didn't waver when the shit hit the fan. The relationships held together by the thread of marital struggle changed or ended. I cut the commonality cord.

I changed.

We get to invite people into our life journey. Not everyone is cut out to be our traveling buddy, and that is perfectly okay. We know who is by the way they show up when we spend time together. We know who is by the unconditional support we feel from them when we struggle. We know who is by the acceptance and normalization they give us. We can be real with them. Not a victim. Not a hero. Just us.

Deep friendships are so important. There's none of that "family" baggage that attaches itself like a leech with blood relations. Friends are the family you get to choose. And true friends are more valuable than gold. They are in your life because you mutually choose each other, not out of duty.

Everyone needs a tribe. They circle when life is hard and surround you with a bulletproof shield. They laugh the kind of laughs that brings tears to your eyes and pee to your pants. They accept who you are and where you've been without question. They know your best self and your worst self. They are expectation-less in their unconditional love.

To be with people who love us in our truth, honesty, bravery, and strength is bliss. To be vulnerable and real and honest and surrounded by protection, respect, and safety is a little glimpse of heaven.

That's what saved my mom.

19

Orphaned at age eighteen, Mom's friends saved her. She took care of her cancer-ridden mother as a young teenager, buried her at sixteen, and grew up way too fast. Christmas Eve two years later, she found her dad dead of a stroke. Left to care for her nine-year-old brother, she vividly remembers hurling the Christmas tree out the front door, ornaments and all.

Without her girlfriends, Mom wouldn't have survived. Friendships matter. Cherish them. Protect them. Familyize them. She passed this onto me and taught me the importance of holding my friends fiercely close. Thank you, Mom.

I'm amazed at the impact and influence mothers have in their families and, most especially, on their daughters. The need to please our mothers is otherworldly and mystical. We mirror and reflect back to them their sense of self. We imitate them. We represent them. We try time after time after time to gain their approval. We want to make them proud of us. If we don't understand them, it messes with us as women.

I knew I was unconditionally loved, but I didn't feel unconditionally accepted as *separate* from her. I think it felt too dangerous, too hard for her to let me be me. I grew up learning that love meant agreement. Always. Have the same opinion as hers. Get hair perms like her. Wear clothes like her. Have views like her. Be her "Mini Me" so that she could feel placement and importance because she grew up with neither.

It makes sense that my mom would pass down her story to me. Moms want what's best for their children. To not suffer or struggle or feel pain. It's in our DNA and instincts. If anyone dares to threaten our children, the mother bear within us rears up and defends our babies to the death. We lift cars off our children. We take bullets for them.

She became the resiliency queen. She had to be. Unable to go to college due to her family situation, Mom says she has a PhD from the School of Hard Knocks. She was the poster child of "Be grateful and thankful and kind." Because "it could always be Much Worse." Choose your view of life. Reframe your circumstances.

My mother and me: bound together forever by our "Glass Half Full" mentality because "it could always be Much Worse." She lived through the Much Worse. She passed down that expertise to me, and I've passed it onto my own children. Thank you, Mom.

Dad was the total and complete opposite of her. Her resiliency was one of the things he loved about her. I'm pretty sure he figured she was strong enough to handle anything he or life threw at her. Yet, I think he longed to have a membership in our exclusive mother-daughter "Glass Half Full" club. But, it didn't match his highly intellectual, fatalistic streak. When I met Bob and said, "I think I met 'the one,' Dad!" he advised me to "Enjoy it now before it bites you in the ass."

He was psychic without knowing it, and maybe that's why he drank.

I remember a day when I traveled to Door County, Wisconsin, with Mom when she was eighty-five. We visited the place of our annual vacations and checked off a bucket-list wish. Her tears hovered near the surface and spilled over as she saw places she never thought she would see again. Memories of the family she created and summers of connection and belonging were almost tangible. The void was filled to the brim with old laughter and new generations and sunsets and sandcastles. Details were blurry now, dates forgotten, but emotions and images razor sharp with connections shared, experiences etched and settled deep in her marrow.

Memories of a time long before me. Gratefulness for her friends and their mothers who rose to fill her emptiness. The ladies of the church, surrogate mothers for her need. Those who anchored her when she wanted no part of her grief-filled life, full of too many losses in too few years.

We sat on a damp bench and watched the sky fade from pink to gray. The drizzly day had cleared in time to paint the sky for us. I touched the bracelet she bought me earlier that day at a store, the name of which escaped her as many things did now. In the dusk, she told me that her parents taught her to lie. Made her say they *needed* to leave her maternal grandmother's house right after they ate dinner. Then they would go to the "fun" side of the family. The place her dad could sing around the piano or spar with his nephew while my mom sat and worried about lying to her grandmother.

"What kind of parent teaches their child to lie?" she asked me in the safety of the dark.

I pieced together the quilt of her childhood. The events and memories that shaped her own motherhood of me. The blurry parts and fuzzy gaps came together with crystal clarity. I finally understood why she needed her things around her. Why receiving cards for her birthday was important and made her feel like she mattered. Why she always sent other people birthday cards. Why she tolerated things I could not. How her need for security and belonging and a place called home was the power behind everything she did.

As I understood her, I understood me.

The influence and importance of a mother is like no other. It doesn't matter if they are alive right now or long dead. Our first sense of who we are comes from them. Our importance and place in this world is defined by them. And theirs was defined by their mother. And that mother was defined by her mother. Since the beginning of time.

And then comes the great separation. We try to figure out where we begin and she ends. We shared bloodstreams with this human being. Took up residence in her body.

How do we filter out the "mom" and leave in the "me"?

20

One of the hardest things you will ever do is to talk to your child about their parent's death. The hardest. Period. The worst thing is to watch your child suffer and not be able to fix it. Sam was eleven when his dad disappeared. He turned twelve the month after we found out Bob had committed suicide. Sam's initial reaction to the five-month-long disappearance was one of complete bafflement, tinged with the fear that his dad would return from wherever he was to hurt us. He worked very hard to make sense of something that wasn't logical in any way. For a long time, Sam played detective in his mind and looked for clues to his dad's behavior.

The day we got the ultimate news, Sam said, "I know this sounds weird, but I'm relieved. We have closure now." I would imagine this is similar to watching a parent suffer with a terminal illness and then die from it. The pain and suffering are over for the beloved parent, but they are gone. Forever. We're relieved that their pain is relieved.

But then our pain replaces that relief very quickly. Sam felt guilty for feeling relieved. I assured him his feelings were completely normal given our situation, and helped him know that he was entitled to feel whatever he was feeling.

During this crazy time of our life, we talked about it whenever HE wanted to. I never forced the conversation, and he picked his times wisely. That I'd asked for a divorce shortly before his dad disappeared complicated things, and as hard as it was for me to hear his anger and pain, I tried to see the situation from his perspective and not take what he said too personally. Sometimes I failed. After all, he'd lost his father. I'd lost my soon-to-be ex-husband. We were in very different places with very different relationships to the very same person that was no longer here.

Recently I asked Sam what he remembered about anything I did that helped him, and now as a wise seventeen-year-old, he said it was good that I let him lead the conversation. That way, he could ask when he had the courage and space to talk about it. Every child is different, and you know yours best. Allow him or her to take the lead and ask questions as they process what happened in pieces, when they are ready. This requires that you do the hard work of being truly present when those times appear. Let them know that their feelings are perfectly understandable. Repeatedly. Even if what they say is painful to hear. Many people are uncomfortable when anger is directed toward the person who is gone, especially when that person died after a valiant battle with a disease. But anger is normal. My son's entire view of his whole life was ripped away, and he is still trying to recreate a future without his dad.

I made sure that Sam had a male therapist to help him wrestle out his feelings, so he could gain a male perspective in his family sea of estrogen. His sixteen-year-old (at the time) sister was in a very different place with vastly different layers to her emotions as she processed her loss. I never wanted either of my kids to feel there was a "right" or "wrong" way to grieve. Instead, I allowed each of them the time and space to feel their feelings. Sam didn't always talk about his dad in his therapy sessions. Sometimes he just talked about "guy stuff," and his therapist filled the role I couldn't. Whether that time was helpful or not, the seeds were planted that it was okay to ask for help to cope with this huge event.

I never felt I needed to be his only source of support. I had to deal with my own emotions around Bob's death and try to honor my grief, as well. If you don't become enmeshed in your child's emotions, you can keep and hold their perspective and contain the hugeness of their grief as they take little bites of it when they have room to digest more.

Be ready for anything. I knew Father's Day would be hard. I knew big events and holidays would be hard. I knew the anniversary of his dad's disappearance would be hard. I prepared for them and gave Sam permission to feel whatever he felt. I acknowledged his pain and told him to be gentle with himself. This is hard, big stuff, and we only know what we know at the time we know it. Your child will grieve in a way that is appropriate for their age and experiences. In Sam's case, the situation was very concrete for him. Dad was simply not here. End of story. What I didn't expect was how long and permanent this grief process would be. I now know it is forever.

As Sam grew, he figured out ways to avoid the pain. He tried hard to diminish the effects of losing his father at eleven. He didn't want to be known as the kid whose father killed himself. So he didn't talk about it for a while. He just wanted to be "normal." Many of his friends didn't even know his story. When they asked, he'd just say, "My dad died." They wouldn't ask, and he wouldn't tell. Your tween may do the same thing. I never pushed him to dig things up and have always believed that we all are on our own grief journeys. No two people deal with loss the same way. But I always gave Sam space to talk on his terms in his own time.

Recently, he admitted he hadn't really dealt with it. But because of the early work we did, Sam was able to ask for help. His maturing mind had struggled long enough alone, and he realized he needed tools he didn't have. He found a safe place to really talk about how he felt now that he had the vocabulary to do so. He says his mind "is cleaner now" that he's been able to articulate what his tween self didn't have the words to express.

And we're still talking ...

21

Father's Day sucks. And it doesn't suck. And sometimes it's both. Every year ... but still ...

The first Father's Day after Bob's suicide was just eight weeks after his memorial service. My kids and I spent it on a boat on Lake Geneva, Wisconsin, with friends. To distract us. How the boat stayed afloat with the huge elephant on it, I'll never know. Still, I'm forever grateful for the friends who chose to be with us and let us bring our elephant along. There was laughter and sunshine ... but still.

The icing on the chaos cake of that first Father's Day was the phone call we received to tell us that my children's beloved Gramma Ginny was very close to death. She died a week later. His mom. Cancer accelerated by a shattered heart. I cannot even fathom her physical and mental pain.

First he left. Then she left. Six weeks between funerals. Two huge losses for my children in rapid succession. And, as much as I tried to deny it, huge losses for me too. Compounded grief ... but still ...

lessons from the ledge

The second year, we went back to Door County, Wisconsin, at the same time we'd always gone as a family in the ***before***. Before our family exploded apart. The kids wanted to go. I wasn't so sure. But if my kids needed to be there, I would take that journey with them. I would help them contain the memories. I would help them confront the ghosts. It sounded like a good idea at the time ... but still ...

This visit included Keith. He lived with us now. He walked the daily tightrope of substitute dad, except not really. He tried to be respectful of the position of Bob and not push. He tried to fill the gap, but still allowed Bob to be present. He tried to let me learn to be both mom and dad while he learned how to be part of our family and find his role. He tried to leave room for the grief without losing his space. Too soon. So hard. Not the timing or way we had planned. Reality borne out of necessity. He left behind an empty job market and daughter in Oregon and moved into a family with a ghost. Door County was his last vacation memory with *his mom* all those years ago. So much grief for all of us ... but still ...

My children have now created their own traditions over these last several Father's Days. One year, they spent the day together over brunch and virgin Bloody Marys to toast their missing person. Without me. He was their dad. Not mine. Their memories. Not mine ... but still ...

I've learned to allow my kids to celebrate, or not, in whatever way feels good and right for them. Some years the day was harder and the celebration quieter. Other years we sat and reminisced about the barbeques, golf games, and the silly cards they gave Bob about farts. Time truly does heal. The pain dulls and the good memories sharpen. Laughter increases and tears decrease ... but still ...

I have no doubt that fathers are important. My children are forever changed. I am forever changed. And yet, we are still here. Thankfully, Father's Day is only one day. It comes and goes in the blink of an eye in whatever form it needs to take from year to year. It never goes by unnoticed. His impact on our lives is never overlooked ... but still ...

Maybe we lone moms should celebrate *us* on that day. Celebrate the amazingly hard job we have to try to be both *father* and *mother* **every day.** Celebrate the house repairs we've learned to make. Celebrate the ability to provide for our families. Alone. Celebrate the gaps we've had to fill. Celebrate the emotions we've learned to contain for our children in their grief. Celebrate the huge impact WE have on our children because we are still here. Celebrate the incredible resiliency we have modeled for our children.

Let's call it Warrior's Day and give ourselves all the love and credit and applause we've earned. And we certainly have EARNED it.

So, on that Sunday in June, Happy Warrior's Day, mothers! Celebrate all that you are. And let Father's Day be whatever it needs to be.

We moms are amazing. Every day. Of every year.

22

Why do some people thrive after trauma and some don't? What is the difference? Upbringing? Attitude? Faith? Support? Drugs? Yoga? Sheer guts? I think it's the ability to reframe.

Try to view your situation, whatever it is, in a positive light. View it through a gratitude lens. Remember, it could always be MUCH WORSE. Look for the lesson in whatever happens. Check your ego at the door and admit you are not in charge—that there's something bigger than our pinhole camera view. There's a panoramic picture we can't see. And just because we can't see it right now doesn't mean it isn't there. Try to think of this as an adventure. Remember that fear and excitement trigger the same response in the body. When I'm about to perform on stage, my stomach gets weird. Some people call it stage fright. Fear. I call it butterflies. Excitement. That was huge for me. Wherever you go, there you are, so you might as well learn to enjoy the roller coaster ride. Or you can grind and grit your teeth and white knuckle it.

Where do you choose to focus? You do have a choice.

Try not to judge what you feel or how you feel it. Why do we believe we need to qualify stuff in black and white terms? Good OR bad? Right OR wrong? Do we do this so we feel we're in control of something? Does judging ourselves equal control? Do we do this so we know how we "should" feel and "should" react? Says who?

Should = (could + shame). It sucks and happens outside of us. Feelings and emotions are not good OR bad. They just are. When I was little, my mom said, "Don't be angry. It's ugly." I heard *"You're ugly."* Now I think I'm pretty damn funny, sexy, and brilliantly powerful when I'm mad. Anger is just one part of me, like any other part.

ALL parts of me are okay. ALL parts of you are okay. ALL parts of us are better than okay. They're magnificent, really.

Energy attracts like energy. What we send out, returns. We all know people who focus on and expect the worst and then seem surprised when it happens. The black cloud follows them everywhere they go because they invited it. We're not powerless in this. We can make a conscious decision to shift from pessimist to optimist. We can learn.

As we learn to reframe and love ourselves, we stretch. When we learn to forgive ourselves when monkey mind moves in and our freak flag flies, the more we connect to ourselves. We're not robots or gurus with all the answers.

lessons from the ledge

We're all flawed and vulnerable and tender and fragile. We're also amazing, strong, and brilliant. We share battle scars from our personal wars and yet fear their exposure. Let's stop pretending we don't all have them, okay? We do. These are the places where the light moves through us. Where we are customized. These are the spots where our souls touch and kiss and embrace and dance together. These are our sacred spots.

Let's try to get off our own backs. Let's try to be real and raw and feel whatever we feel. Notice I said "try." It's a process. It's a conscious choice. It's a concerted effort. And it's important.

23

When tragedy strikes, friends, family and even strangers feel the need to say something, anything to us. Well intentioned and uncomfortable, they try to lessen our pain and find some comfort for us AND them. They offer platitudes, and that gets old really fast in the midst of crisis.

People care, and we get that they want to help ease our pain. I appreciate their intention and desire to offer comfort, but it makes me want to shout, "Please save the sayings and give *yourself*!"

This is what I heard and what I struggled to appreciate:

"I'm praying for you." First of all, how many times do we say we'll do something and then forget to do it? It's human nature. Life and busyness get in the way. We meant it when we said it. We really did. But then we forgot. So don't just throw that out there to have something to say. Pray for me first and then tell me you did.

"Everything happens for a reason." Be prepared for

pushback on this one. Because I believe in God, I believe that someday I'll understand how all the puzzle pieces fit together. Someday. But right now? Sometimes tragedies happen because someone made a horrible choice. When a drunk driver kills your loved one, the reason is because they made a horrible decision to drive drunk. Or someone got a horrible incurable disease. What's the reason for that? And to someone who doesn't believe in God, this platitude rings hollow and offers little comfort. Or even causes more damage.

"God never gives you more than you can handle." Sometimes shit just happens. Someone rejects us or abuses us or we lose our job or someone dies. We all make mistakes that have consequences attached. God doesn't sit up in his puppet booth in the sky and say, "Hmmm, Nancy needs to be stronger, so I'm going to make her husband disappear and then kill himself. And then, I'm going to continually throw hard things her way so that she will know she can handle things. And then when I think she has handled enough and proven how strong she is, I'll stop." If you think that phrase pisses *me* off, try it on someone who's lost a child. That is not how my God works. It's just not.

"Let me know if I can do anything." Please don't tell me this. I have no clue what you can do. I have no clue what I even need. I'm already overwhelmed, and the last thing I need is to try and figure out a job for you. Just do something. Anything. Surprise me. I'm pretty sure I will be grateful for whatever it is.

So what can you say?

A simple "I'm sorry," "I'm here," "I have no words," or even "This sucks," is honest. It's real. It's true. It doesn't try to fix the situation because the situation is unfixable. You know it. I know it. So, let's not pretend.

Just give us you.

24

When loss smacks you in the face, you find out fast that you're made of some pretty tough stuff and you're capable of some pretty incredible things. You survive in ways you never thought you could, because you have to. You find out fast where to focus your limited energy. No more wasted time and brain space on what other people think because your jig is up and your imperfect life is exposed. Platitudes hold no comfort but *real* becomes gold.

It sounds weird, but I found it freeing.

No more pretending.

Be prepared that your new *real* may make other people very uncomfortable with this newfound transparency. Especially if they are still caught up in what other people think. But that's okay. Let them squirm. Let them be uncomfortable. That is about them. Not you. They own it. You don't.

Stay in the present as best you can, but if you slip and wander into the scary, dark future, oh well. We all do. Take yourself to that worse case future scenario, but ask a new question: "How likely is that to happen? Really?" Then breathe yourself back into *your now*. When we're stressed, we leave ourselves behind and go to places in our heads we don't yet belong. We hold our breath and starve ourselves of oxygen, and then hyperventilate and panic. Stop it, already! Breathe!

Remember you ALWAYS have choices. I repeat: You always have choices! You may feel like you don't, but you do. In each moment, you can choose how to show up and how to respond. Or not. And you can be okay with not responding because you're just too damn tired and need a nap. Or a good cry.

Trust that you'll know what you need to know when you need to know it. You know?

Feelings are not reality, and they are not good or bad. It's the value WE put on them that makes them so. Don't judge them. They exist. They're what make us human. We're bigger than they are, and feelings can't kill us. It might feel like we will die of sadness, but it isn't true. What is true is that we will never have this moment again. What is true is that our feelings will change, and we'll have new ones in new moments. They will ebb and flow like the tide.

So ride the wave, my friend, with gentleness, love, and understanding.

Personalize your grief process. It's yours. Own it. Don't try to fit into anyone else's experience and stop gauging where you are in Kubler-Ross's stages. Just be. Feel what you feel. Allow other people to grieve in their own way on their own timeframe, too. Hold that space for them gently. Fiercely. Each person's connection to loss is uniquely theirs.

My children processed the loss of their father in very different ways on uncoordinated timeframes. I didn't judge the ways they coped and came to terms with life without Bob. I acknowledged the deepness of their pain. That soothed them and grew me. It forced me to see the limits of my control and to sit in my "I can't fix this" chair and get comfortable and settled in it.

They are both warriors in their own ways on their own paths. Sometimes they ask me to join them, and we talk together as they move along. Other times, they head off individually or together as siblings to experience this unasked-for adventure. Either way, we stop and start and rock and roll. It is what it is, and we all try to stay present and not judge ourselves or each other for where we are in any given moment.

But it's hard. We know it and acknowledge it.

Transitions and grief are a messy and imperfect process. We're all trailblazers on this path. And everyone is so very different. When I start to second guess myself or feel the fake trying to reimplant again with the inevitable "I should …" I ask myself the question, "Says who?" If the answer belongs to anyone but me, if it is the world or my friends or the ever present "Should" Society, I let it go. Those are old echoes of someone else's story. Not mine.

When we can be present enough to stop and listen to our own heart and trust our intuition, we're real. We return. Peace returns. Remember this is a lifelong learning curve. We've never done this moment before. Our "now" isn't in the damn brochure.

There is no brochure. *THERE IS NO INSTRUCTION MANUAL!*

When big stuff happens, some people leave. They can't fix it. And that sucks. They want the suck to stop, so they try to muscle the situation into something they CAN fix. The griever ends up feeling "less than" and the loss gets downplayed. And, guess what? It still can't be fixed. So, if those people have to go, let them. Grieve yet another loss and open up the space for new people.

And learn. Always learn.

25

If we don't take the time and space we need to grieve, it settles into our nooks and crannies. Grief is an attention whore, and she screams to be heard and acknowledged. If we don't listen, it festers. It spreads and infects us. It defines us and colors the way we see the world. It throws us off balance. It spews out through our cracks and hits everyone around us.

I knew it was time two years after. It had to happen. I've always been a delayed reactor. It takes me time to slow down and feel my feelings. Eventually, my distraction and procrastination expertise expires. I own this about myself. It was time. To be still, to stop running, to mourn the past. To contemplate and journal and reflect. To sit in my grief space.

That space is where I began to miss Bob. To refresh perspective. To miss aspects of my old life with him. And appreciate him. Truly. I found clear room to honor what he did well and to rekindle the compassion that had been snuffed out. There were days I realized how afraid he must have been. How much pressure he must have felt to provide for us. That was how he showed us he loved us. Maybe it's why he wouldn't share our financial situation. That was his love "job," and to share it might lessen his importance. He didn't want a partner.

Bob couldn't see that being a team multiplies. It doesn't subtract.

It was in this space where my story grew flesh. Where I began to get my new balance. To get my sea legs and core—*true core*—engaged, so I could roll with these new life waves. The old stiff stance I took that got me knocked down by the big swell of "What the hell?" faded. It was hard and some days I just needed to do nothing. Some days, the grief waves got too strong, so I'd distract myself and berate myself for being weak and needy and unproductive. My one "down" day would grow into three or four as I energetically assaulted myself.

But I still learned. And I still grew.

Grief is tricky. It lies calmly right below the surface most of the time. But some days? Even when you think you have done everything to prepare for that holiday season, anniversary, birthday, reminder of vacancy, grief can roar to the surface. The anticipation of these significant days is far more difficult than the actual day itself.

Ride the wave as it comes and know the wave eventually takes you to shore. Feel it. Acknowledge it. Grief stays in your face until you do. You'll get through it and grief will settle down and go back to its rightful place. But it will never go away.

Time has a way of softening its hard edges. It creates something new and beautiful in its place. Like beach glass. It creates space so there's more time to regain your balance and catch your breath in between those tsunamis. Raging grief hurricanes eventually become tropical grief storms, spring grief rain, and, eventually, gentle grief showers.

And through it all, you must LEARN TO TAKE CARE OF YOU! In an emergency, flight attendants tell you to put on your oxygen mask first before you help those around you. If you don't take care of yourself, you cannot take care of anyone else. This was a hard lesson for me and ran counter to all the "shoulds" in my life around marriage and motherhood.

This promotion from last to first place was a tough sell and a hard climb. "If Momma ain't happy, ain't nobody happy!" I hadn't been happy for a long time; HOWEVER I was really, really good at the creation of happy for everyone else. When I stopped the happy manufacture, I realized my kids hadn't learned to make it for themselves. Their happiness muscles were weak and they couldn't fly. I had done too much to open their cocoons for them and deprived them of the need to work for their wings. My good intentions and discomfort with unhappy had crippled my children. Their struggle reminds me daily that my fake almost killed them. They looked to me to rescue them, make the hard way easier, even though they know "No pain, no gain." They now know they have to figure it out and do their own work. And they are. Inch by inch some days, mile by mile others.

We are created for relationships. Wired to connect. Wired to grieve losses as a process of humanness. If you stuff your emotions or deny grief its place in your life, it lessens the impact of that relationship you lost, of that person. Makes it seem like the loss didn't matter. Like it was cheap and we can always just go buy another whatever it was. Remember, you are the boss of your grief trip. There is no right or wrong way to travel. It belongs to you. And only you.

Trust yourself. Love yourself. Be gentle and show yourself the same compassion and safety you'd give everyone else. Maybe grief tries to re-anchor us to our best, most raw real, and that's why it hurts. We get stripped down to our naked selves and we are at our most vulnerable, our most beautiful human imperfection, so we understand we are powerless. But we aren't. We are real. And we have choices.

People have an expectation of grief. Like there's a timeframe for it. You get this many months and then you should snap out of it and move on. Other people do. Life goes on. Seasons change. Holidays and anniversaries come and go. Kids graduate. Milestones happen. Life happens. Get over it. Like it's a challenge course in boot camp with that big wall at the end when you're

lessons from the ledge

exhausted. If you can just get over that wall, you're at the finish line. Except we know nobody gets over that wall alone. They get over that wall with the help of those who have already finished the course.

But grief? It's an unending boot camp, so we rest up as best we can and set off again. Together.

Others who haven't experienced a loss are afraid to talk about it with those who have. Like grief is contagious. We all will experience loss of some kind. No one lives forever. None of us get out of life alive. Grief is an inevitable part of life and yet no one wants to talk about it. It's put away in the closet of our minds until, one day, someone dies or leaves or suffers an illness or accident or loss that changes life forever. The closet door gets flung open.

Grief is lonely. Seek solace with people who understand and aren't afraid to talk about it. To feel it with you. To experience it with you. To sit smack dab in the middle of it with you. Who accept that grief is a normal response to the loss of someone or something really important.

Elizabeth Kubler-Ross tried to put grief into manageable, measurable stages. This way, we can "know" where we are and when we'll be "done," right? We are people who like answers, timeframes, and neat packages all tied with bows. We accept her research and there is much that is good in it. However, I think that's where a lot of our expectations come from. Her work focused on the ones who were dying. For them, there is finality. Those of us left behind know that we're never done. We are never over it. There is nothing final about it. Instead, we're changed. Everything is changed. And we're here in unfamiliar territory, trying to find our new way. We're still alive, but with a permanent void.

Maybe grief isn't talked about in polite company because it is uncontrollable. We didn't choose the event. We didn't choose the outcome. It wasn't our choice or timeframe or circumstance, and we get reminded that we don't control much, if anything, in life. But we can control one thing—how we choose to respond. It takes a strong person to show up in grief. To ride the wave and sometimes get buried by it. But sometimes, we ride it to the top of the swell and can be amazed by the view from up there. There can be joy in grief. It's okay. It really is. It isn't disloyal or weird or inappropriate.

Grief reminds us there are no guarantees in life. We don't take relationships or life or love or beauty or pain or joy for granted anymore. We slow down and notice because we know these things won't be noticeable forever. We are more *present* in this moment because we know no other moments are promised. We worry less and love more. We hold on to others more loosely to allow them to flourish instead of choke-holding them in our fist of fear, afraid to lose them.

Grief is intimately personal. It is as different and unique as we are as individuals. We all grieve differently;

it hits us at different times and for different reasons. It takes time for the sharpness of its edges to wear down. Don't judge those who grieve. Unique grief belongs to each of us. I don't say, "I know how you feel" because I don't. Neither do you.

Grief is hard work. Mentally and physically. Our brains start a process to try to determine which memories are the most important to keep. Like when we sort through thousands of pictures and divide them into "keep" and "toss" piles. Awake or asleep, our brains try to fill the huge, gaping vacuum.

Grief can't be fixed. My job as Supermom and Superwife was to make everyone else happy, comfortable, and safe. To be the fixer. Bob's death taught me about unfixable things. No matter how "super" I thought I was, this was my kryptonite. I hate that I can't make it all better. It is unspeakably hard to watch those I love struggle and hurt. But in reality, fixing was never my job anyway. Now no one has to pretend anymore. It is what it is.

> Promise me you'll always remember: You're braver than you believe, and stronger than you seem, and smarter than you think.
> — A. A. Milne

26

The Grief Möbius

Wikipedia says, "a Möbius strip is made with a piece of paper and tape. If an ant were to crawl along the length of this strip, it would return to its starting point having traversed the entire length of the strip (on both sides of the original paper) without ever crossing an edge."

When we lose someone or something significant, and we all do eventually, we're told we "should" move on. And we do. But not like they want us to. Our grief runs in the background like the location on our phone … it always knows where we are. It uses up batteries and data space. We're on the Möbius strip of life, missing that person. Forever. We move along. In our own way. In our own time. We do the best we can. And then …

We're back at the beginning. Except the beginning moved. It's not in the same place, but it may feel just hard as it did the first time. But a different "hard." In any given moment, we grieve. It's part of us now, this grief, as much a part of us as our phones or our limbs.

The speed we travel the Möbius strip varies. Sometimes, we crawl along by inches and our viewpoint barely changes. Sometimes, we fly around the strip quickly, experiencing highs and lows in an hour or a day. Sometimes, we spend a season of the year on the underside of the Möbius strip. Or a significant date comes up and down we go.

Eventually, every moment isn't hard. But initially? Brutal. Brutal. Brutal. All the "firsts" in our unrequested, redecorated life. All the furnishings moved without our opinion or our permission. Nobody asked us what we wanted to get rid of or send to storage. It just happened. Something disappeared. Someone is missing. Everything is just off. Way off. We adjust to this new room arrangement because we have to learn to get used to it.

But we always have choices. We *could* stick our feet into wet denial concrete and let it harden. We *could* decide to be the victim of our unfortunate circumstance. We *could* wear the distinction proudly as a badge that defines us. But that really only hurts us in the short and long run and keeps us stuck.

Grief denied oozes out the sides and will spew over everything. It demands our attention. It denies our pain and suffering. It is fake and small and harmful. And when we become a victim, we become fake and small and harmful.

So we adapt. We work nonstop, consciously AND unconsciously to integrate this new view. We travel the grief Möbius strip. We recreate a future missing someone or something. We accept that everything we thought we knew is different now.

We can't phone it in. We have to show up in the process. We have to be present every moment. It is necessary.

So we navigate this Möbius strip. And just when we think we're getting somewhere, we end up, once again, at the starting point. Or what feels like the starting point. But, THIS TIME, as we integrate and internalize this new "living room" arrangement, even though we may feel like we're going backwards, it's actually a new starting point. THIS TIME, we have more energy and less fear because we've been here before, and we know we can do this. Because we ARE doing this.

We've teetered on the strip edge, but never crossed it. We've been on the side facing down and seen things that broke our hearts with sorrow. We've been on the up side and seen things that filled our hearts with joy. We've sprinted and we've sat. That's this grief life of ours.

The secret is to look around and see. The secret is to trust that wherever we are, we are just fine. We are doing the very best we can. Every passing day, week, and year, even moment, offers a new vantage point and view. From wherever we are on the Möbius strip of grief.

27

According to the *Oxford Dictionary,* validation is "The feeling of recognition from others that you are right or good enough." This need controls us, and we hand over our power willy-nilly to those we think will pat us on the head.

I've done it for years. I've looked for approval—usually from males—and now I look back and see a lot of wasted time. Time spent feeling powerless. Time spent waiting. Waiting for that pat on the head and "Atta girl" from Guy Du Jour.

The irony is that most people don't want our power. They don't ask for it. We hand it over and thrust it mentally onto them, whether they're up for it or not. Whether they're equipped to be healthy power holders or not. Then we get hurt, disappointed, even angry that they don't take tender loving care of our unasked for power gift. Worse yet, they don't take tender loving care of us. That's our job.

Ever had someone tell you something so deep, so heavy, so personal that you didn't know what to do with it? You thought, "Wow. I really didn't want to know that. Why are you telling me this? I didn't ask for turbo intimacy. What do I do now?"

Awkward.

Be careful! When we allow someone else to become the mirror of how we view ourselves, we better do some research to determine if theirs is cracked. Or warped. Or true. Ever stand in front of a mirror that you know adds ten pounds to your reflection? Or makes you look taller than you actually are? It isn't your true reflection but you accept it.

As long as we look for validation from other people, we will always be under their power. We hope they will fight for us, put effort into our fulfillment and happiness, and give us enough of something, anything to fill our "not enough" void.

They didn't ask for our power. They didn't ask to be our mirror. Sometimes they don't even know what to do with their own power. Sometimes, they are unable to see themselves in their own mirrors.

Wise words from Shakespeare (emphasis mine):

> This above all: to thine **own** self be true.

28

Guilt is stupid. It keeps us small. It keeps us stuck. It goes against the belief that every decision, every path we choose, leads to where we are at this moment. It robs our lives of sacredness. It confuses us, pisses us off, and makes us do stupid stuff.

After Bob left, even before, even always, guilt was pretty constant in my life. I felt guilty when I was home. *I should be at work.* I felt guilty when I was away. *I should be home, being the perfect mother.* I felt guilty when I felt small. *I should measure up.* How? Measure up to what? I felt guilty for feeling guilty.

Guilt is the cousin of shame, and the twin of should. They all show up at the same time. They like to hang out together. I think they're all stupid.

My relationship with my children leaned toward being an equal or a friend. Cool mom. Please Like Me! Please Like Me! Validate me because God knows your dad sure can't, so now it's your job! They were my world. There wasn't much emotional attachment with Bob, so I sucked on them like a leech, trying to satisfy my need for a fix of connection, for conversation, for coolness.

I know so many women whose lives revolve around their children, until the moods, triumphs, and struggles of their kids become their own. Their popularity, talent, and grades are all a reflection and possession of their awesome mother. I get it. It may work for a while, but it doesn't work forever.

The legend of the perfect mom came from somewhere. Maybe it came from the media, from comparisons to other moms or my own mom's example. As I slowly excavate the artifacts of that perfection story, I will continue to understand and grow.

Once I became a stay-at-home mom with a work-from-home husband, I felt I should earn my unemployed existence. Keeping humans alive every day wasn't any big deal, right? I was lucky to be allowed to stay home, so I knew I better be grateful every second of every day. And I better make everything I do look effortless in my invisible Donna Reed pearls, while they choked the life out of me. I played the role of "The Nurturing Whore Maid" well and took the bait, hook-line-sinker-guilt. I swallowed the role whole, drawing it deep into my marrow. It felt right. So easy. So familiar. And yet—

Eventually I came up for air and I realized that guilt got me nowhere. Shame kept me small and fake. It kept me safe. Low expectations for my life. Riskless. All I had to do was memorize the lines for my role. Parrot back what I'd been taught to believe I was. And keep the face on. Smile. Keep the house picked up and the dinner hot. Be whatever anyone needed me to be. At any time. In any place. I gave away my power to everyone around me. Whether they wanted it or not.

It isn't always pretty, but my kids and I have a high level of honesty and the ability to repair fast. We cut each other slack most of the time, but sometimes we slice and dice each other with our words as we navigate this new threesome family.

At the start of all of this, Sam's therapist told the three of us, "Wow. You all just let your emotions fly and hit the walls, whatever you're feeling, with no regard to who gets splattered in the process."

"Well, at least we're honest," I replied.

"Brutally," he said.

We laugh big. We cry big. We love big.

Bad Day—A Journal Entry
2015

I feel like such a pretender. Losing fake footing and celebrating fake sanity. Looking for numbness because reality is just too damn hard. Distracting myself from the way things are by getting involved in things to forget. Reverting back to setting my needs and desires on the back burner to balance everyone else's expectations and needs and pain. Kidding myself that someday we will all be whole again and happy in our lives. Productive and pain free. Never really finding resolution to this minor chord—just dark, discordant, disconnected doom.

My family is in shambles. My happiness gets stolen, or do I hand it over willingly? My daughter hates me at times, and sometimes it's pretty mutual. It's so hard and I don't know what to do. Again, it wasn't in the brochure. I know plenty of people who struggle with their kids with far less catastrophe than we've had. The anger is right below the surface, like a pressure cooker ready to blow. And it does. Often. It is really tricky, this surviving suicide. The wound is deep and never heals. Moving forward is hard and complicated and brittle. Shaky steps forward and huge miles backward, this ebb and flow of grief. And it can be nasty. Dark. Always lurking, waiting to steal our happy. Festering. Powerful. Mean.

I feel attacked and sucked dry. I work so hard to take care of myself. Protect myself. I asked for it, I suppose. I stopped the fake, and yet it rears its ugly head time and time and time again. It's hard to be mad at a ghost. The tragic victim or the perpetrator?

lessons from the ledge

Which one is it? Is he? I'm left with a big pile of ugly to try to sort through. To search for some little nugget of good in all of it. The heavy, heavy baggage left for me to sort out and own and to figure out how to go forward into a future that, in that moment in my heart, I know I can't win. I'm powerless and answerless. It's just too heavy to bear so often, and I'm just tired. Deep in my bones tired and worn out from wishing and hoping and dreaming that life will somehow be different. Better. But maybe this is just the way it will always be. Lost and anchorless and tossed all over the place, from bad to worse, back to bad. Maybe the moments of okayness are just creations of my crazy mind.

There aren't enough words, they haven't been invented yet, don't exist to describe the depth and breadth of every cell screaming in pain of what is left now. How much can people take? How can something affect every aspect of our lives from finances to relationships to education to futures imagined? Trying something, anything, everything I know in my mind and heart and experience to make life okay again. To make it normal, mundane. Instead, every moment is sharp and pointy and painful and hard and heavy. There are too many dark days.

I tried to convince myself that five long years is a milestone of survival. A huge anniversary to be celebrated because we are all still here. The worst is now behind us, and good things are ahead. But where's my "time heals" breakthrough? How to describe that if things hadn't changed, I wouldn't be here? I would have ended my life because I felt already dead. God, that sounds so melodramatic, but it is my truth in this moment. No way out. No way to escape the journey I had a hand in. Where's my medal of survival? My reward? My kudos for grief containment for my kids while grappling with my own on a daily, hourly basis? I knew early on that I would be the target of their anger and the punching bag for their deep, deep hurt. It's hard to be angry with a dead man. It feels insulting and petty and wrong because a ghost cannot defend itself.

Throw in menopause, and it is one big emotional amusement park roller coaster full of family fun.

Guilt is stupid. It keeps me small.

29

I've tried and tried to wrap my brain around budgets and finances. That old "I need a man to do this" voice is taking its sweet time to fade. But I keep at it and try to learn new stuff about me. Somehow the bills get paid, and life gets lived.

When I got married, I felt an immense sense of relief. Someone else could deal with the money stuff. *Take care of me! Waahh! I don't like this part of grownup-hood. I just want to spend money and never think about it! But I like the challenge of a good deal! Never pay full price! I like new things! I want to look cute and up to date! If people admire my style, I want to tell them the deal I got, so they think I'm okay! But I don't want to think about it!*

Bob used to tease me that he paid a $5,000 dowry for me. I had racked up some credit card debt, and he took over the payments after we married. When I think back, I still feel my body tense up today. It was a big deal. That dowry "joke" got weaponized, usually used with some connection to what I'd spent, earned, or why I couldn't be trusted with the financial part of our family. I brushed it off but buried it deep.

That dowry joke fit the message I'd accepted about myself, as evidenced by the grades I'd earned in math, and it kept me a little girl. I was that little girl for a very long time. Long after the dependence served me. I never brought up the higher cost of our car insurance, his legal bills, the family sacrifices we made, so he could run his own business. I tried so hard to be kind and loving. I really did.

I wonder if Bob thought I would blow it—this life after suicide. Would I bring the family to its financial knees, lose the house, file for bankruptcy? Maybe he felt I'd be okay—we'd be okay—because he'd left us enough to be okay. Because he had worked so hard, for so long, to provide for us.

What is it about money that turns me into a little, helpless girl again? That voice of "you're nothing without a man" was out in the open now. So I decided to learn about the psychological power of money in my life. For the first time, I saw the depth of loneliness and fear my mom must have felt when her parents died. That she wanted to keep me safe and protect me from living her experience. I made that nagging voice my ally. Began to see it as a well-intentioned protector instead of my enemy. It shrunk in size and power and a new, strong voice began to grow in volume. My voice.

This financial outlook is a one step forward, three steps back trail to blaze. Since Bob left, I've lost a lot of my capacity to retain information. I've read very few books from cover to cover, and don't have time for fiction. So I filled my email inbox with inspirational and positive articles. That's how I found Kate Northrup. I love her energy, humor, and openness. I started to follow her blog and loved how easy it was to connect to her. I liked her attitude, outlook and her "real." Her book, *Money: A Love Story*, spoke to me in a way nothing else had and I thought, *If anyone can make sense of this for me, it's her.*

Her book changed me. It was the first time I heard money talked about from a spiritual/psychological side, and I was hooked. I devoured the book. Cover to cover. My thoughts around money changed, the fear died down, and I adopted an attitude of prosperity. Kate's book helped me reframe my deepest fear. I'm not perfect at it, but I've come a long way, Baby! I had a moment of *Aha* and realized that all our struggles come from a lack of self-love, and it opened my eyes to a whole new world of compassion. For everyone. But most of all, for me. I'm not an idiot. Nobody else thinks I'm an idiot. But I told myself I was an idiot. Repeatedly. I was so mean to me. With Kate's positive mojo that labeled bills "Invoices for Blessings Already Received"—well, it clicked. It was financial truth with a positive, slightly "woo-woo" twist that I loved. And it was from a woman. Not another male voice in my head that looked at the *problems* of making ends meet, sticking to a budget, and just NOT spending ANY money. No frustration toward me when I couldn't grasp a concept the way it was presented. But rather a funny, high-energy girlfriend who introduced the concept of choice, gratitude, and relationship with money. I moved from a fear of "lack" to embracing an "abundance" mindset. I faced down fear, and I know I am blessed beyond measure. And I know that is powerful. I will always have enough. Because I AM enough.

Thank you, Kate.

30

The first Christmas Bob was missing and we didn't know from minute to minute what the hell was going on, I took my kids to downtown Chicago overnight. It was time to create some new traditions, whether Bob showed up ever again or not. The change of scenery, a dip in an indoor pool, and the energy of the Christmas lights and shoppers on Michigan Avenue proved to be a nice distraction from our crazy. We did that for the first two years without Bob. Then life gained speed; I went to work, Jill was in college and then Europe the next year, so it just slipped down the priority list. Now it's a nice, new memory in a sea of hard, old ones.

Every holiday. Every birthday. Every milestone. There's this palpable crackle of fragile because Bob isn't here. Emotions perch on the edge to jump off at a second's notice. Someone is missing. Celebrations take more effort. I used to be tired because "back then," I did everything all by myself, and I'd be angry and resent Bob. Resentment and anger are such energy suckers. And holidays are hard for lots of people, catastrophes or not. Now I have to dig deeper to find that holiday reserve. Jill and Sam are older, so their excitement and anticipation that used to fuel me aren't quite the same. There are more financial constraints, and everything is still on me. Holidays compared to "before" and "after" can make me feel like I'm a failure in the present. Or that I failed in the past. Or just failed. Period.

Most of the time, I can dodge the failure arrows, but there are times when I'm struggling (which children do not understand … I am not allowed to remove my superhero cape, not even to get it dry cleaned) and those arrows hit their mark. They stir up that big old crockpot of simmering guilt, shame, and "shoulds" that is usually kept in the corner of my head.

Weddings suck now. I wish they didn't. I miss the joyful tears. When that father walks that daughter down the aisle? The father-daughter dance? That kills me. I get so sad.

Then I get pissed.

And that's okay.

31

Work on forgiveness. Forgive yourself. Forgive the circumstance. Forgive the relationship. Forgive the universe. Forgive. It's hard but necessary work and is the way to keep from getting hard and bitter yourself. It's a process. Do it and trust it.

I trust it. But I don't like it. At all. It's too hard sometimes, and I get stuck. I know all about the importance of forgiveness. I know that holding grudges is unhealthy and will take its toll. If you don't forgive, you allow that other person to keep your power, and I know that's true. Many things I've read, especially with a religious bent, put conditions around forgiveness and made me feel like I wasn't a "good" Christian because I still struggle with it. Even years later, I think forgiveness is so hard and consuming and repetitive because it reminds us how human and fallible we all are. It reminds me that I need to seek the divine within myself to release my white-knuckled grip on Bob over and over and over again. The hard work of forgiveness keeps me connected to my best, most real me. The one God made.

Maybe forgiveness isn't something to be grinded out, worked on, struggled with. Maybe it happens with more stillness and gentleness, gradually, when we aren't even aware. Maybe it works over time in secret to deepen my understanding of the person I need to forgive, which all too often is me.

As I learn to forgive myself, grief grows me in unexpected ways. Letting myself off the hook is the ultimate act of self-love when monkey mind takes hold and up goes my freak flag for all to see. I'm not a robot or a guru with all the answers. I'm flawed and vulnerable and tender and fragile. I value people when they share their flaws and fears because we all have them. I understand we are not alone. We ALL have those terrifying moments of uncertainty that make us human. Cracks in our veneer where the light moves into and out of us. The sacred places where our souls touch and kiss and embrace and dance together in real.

And that's where the bliss is.

A high school friend of mine got cancer. The old me would have run from his terminal diagnosis. The new me leaned into that friendship. The new me acknowledged the pain and called it what it was. The new me knew it would hurt like hell when he died. And it did. And it does. Loss is hard. Separation sucks. But I stored up memories to recall.

I learned about true love, even when it's really, really hard. I met his wife, who said "I do" with full knowledge of the repercussions of a short life lived in sickness, not health. Her bravery and embrace of that love astounded me. I'll forever remember the talks with my friend where we were real.

And then there was Keith. To let go of him was one of the hardest things I've ever done. After he'd moved in with us and we'd made wedding plans, the decision to send him on his way was bigger and scarier than everything about Bob. I was so programmed to depend on a man that the thought of being alone terrified me. But I knew then, and now, that it was necessary. I had started to shrink again. Felt the familiar eggshells under my feet, and the fists starting to clench, ready to defend. I tried to convince myself that it didn't matter, that we had the rings, the date, the dress, tux, and reception site. That I loved him. But I knew to truly heal and find me, I had to go it alone. I had to trust my gut. I couldn't juggle the needs of Keith and the needs of my kids. And the needs of me weren't even important enough to be put into the rotation. By me. Again. I was doing it again.

Except this time, I recognized it. I felt it. I acknowledged it. And I put an end to it.

The day he left, I went to a new Starbucks to do some work on my coaching program. I had just finished my BA (with support and encouragement from Keith) and was considering a master's degree. My therapist was the one who urged me to get my coaching certification.

"With what you've been through, there are so many areas you could focus on to coach others."

I trusted her words. As I sat reading a book for the program, I tried to digest that my future with Keith was over. Ended by me. Again. My soul mate had driven south to Atlanta, and I was still here. Sad and excited at the same time.

"We'll need a speaker for that date," I heard from the table next to me. I felt a cosmic nudge, and a voice in my head said, *If you don't do this, you'll regret it the rest of your life.* I faced down my fear, and I realized I could go to a lot of other Starbucks if I humiliated myself at this one. What did I have to lose?

"I don't mean to interrupt, but I overheard you say you were looking for a speaker?" I plopped my new business card on the table before they could protest. "I AM a speaker and coach. Here's my card."

They booked me on the spot. The executive committee for a B2B (Business to Business) network that was connected to the Chamber of Commerce gave me a chance. My life busted open that day, and I have never looked back. The people from that group soon became my insurance rep, my financial planner, my website designer, the first person to publish my writing, my mechanic, and my AAA guy. They were my confirmation that I was going to be just fine on my own.

And I am.

32

One day, out of nowhere, full-on bliss hit me. A sense of overwhelming aliveness. I had to cry to release some of it, or I would have burst wide open. Gutted by gratitude. My only response was "Thank you!" and I said it over and over again in my blissful bathroom. It was the only prayer I needed for the overflowing contentment that I am who I was created to be.

Finally.

I have no idea what triggered this particular moment of exultation, but I'm so glad I didn't miss this bliss. I'm sure there have been other moments, but many times, especially when I was focused on the facade, I missed them. Distracted by destructing myself. Sidetracked by the to-do lists of "should." This time I was present enough, aware enough, to let it wash over me.

My out-of-body bliss moment didn't last long in its intensity, but the memory hung around all day. I don't think I could've survived that intense level for an extended period. That fullness. Floating above myself, bursting with peace and contentment.

Later that week, as I was headed to the Pilsen neighborhood in Chicago on the EL train, a fellow rider shared the story of his "angel" mom's death to ovarian cancer with me. Total strangers, we shared a sacred moment. Why he opened up to me that day, I'll never know. His story etched him into my life through his honesty and pain and joy and appreciation of all she had poured into his life. He blessed me. Literally. We connected so deeply in those moments that it took my breath away and brought tears to my eyes. A total stranger, yet I knew him. And he poured out his grief from years ago. But it wasn't sad. It was poignant. It was tender. It was beautiful with the patina that comes from keeping something near, where it can be touched all the time.

I will never forget him, his deep love and admiration for her, and his courage to be real with me.

Bliss can be invited. But it can't be controlled. It's in plain sight and hidden. Mysterious, but normal. If you try too hard to control situations, outcomes, or people, bliss will hide from you. But when let go, bliss will visit. And once it does, you want more.

You become addicted.

Bliss addiction.

33

Dear Humanity

Let's make a pact right now to rock our lives and this planet. No more living "beige." No more just getting by. No more gritting our teeth Sunday night to grind through the workweek. No more spending precious, limited energy on living a life of "less than."

Life is short and goes so fast, and we spend a lot of it on the ledge. When we're born, we're a bundle of energy. Shiny. Untarnished. Unlimited. Glorious potential. Perfectly designed to do something in life that is uniquely ours.

We grow up and travel our life path. Sometimes fast. Sometimes slow. We gain experience as we wander through "our field" until one day, something big happens that stops us in our tracks. Something big happens that opens our eyes. Maybe it's sickness or disease. Maybe it's death or divorce. Maybe it's unemployment or eviction. Or maybe it's an unrelenting, nagging feeling that life is flying by, and we're really not soaring.

We look at ourselves for the first time in a long time, or maybe ever, and see that we are covered in burrs and thorns. The brambles and thistles we've wandered through in "our field" have stuck to us. *What the hell? Where'd they come from? How'd they get there?"* we wonder.

And that's our work. Figure out where they came from and how they got there. Did we accidently brush against a bramble, or did someone push us into it? Did we jump head first into the thorn bush? The flowers looked so pretty at the time …

So, we start the work of our life. We pull off those burrs, one by one. Pull out the uninvited thorns that have embedded in us. We examine them. Assumptions we've internalized. Interpretations stuck to us. Limitations we gathered like badges on a sash. People told us to stick some on, so we would look just like everybody else. Judgment poked us and stayed.

We might remember the initial pain when some of them stuck. "That was the thorn bush I fell into. I scrambled out of it, but I was a bloodied mess. I remember!" More often, we don't realize that we are gathering a collection. One burr can be pretty stealthy. But when we gather enough, we move a certain way and OUCH! We feel them. We look down at ourselves and realize we're covered with them.

If we're honest and stop long enough, we realize those burrs have slowed us down. They've robbed our joy.

They've stolen our energy. They've distracted us and kept us small, and our lives bore us to tears now. That's why so many of us never stop to look. We don't want to know. We run through "our field" and ignore the pain. We don't want to deal with our thorns. We don't want to do our life work. Until something big happens, and we're forced to stop running.

Is this work hard? You bet.

Is it necessary? You know it.

Is it worth it? Absolutely.

And if we do it, we will change the world.

acknowledgments

Every good story has a beginning, middle, and end. Yet this story goes on and will until my last breath. Tragedy and triumph, bruises and badges, lows and highs. This book wrote me as I wrote it and the following pivotal people are so important that "thank you" just doesn't cut it. From my bottomless heart, you have my undying gratitude …

~ Robert D. Nelson, father of our children and my accidental teacher
~ Joan Strickland, my mom and biggest influence
~ Jillian Nelson, my daughter, my world changer, who is so very brave
~ Sam Nelson, the wisest young man I am privileged to call son
~ Keith Amber, my soul mate
~ Melissa Berler, my therapist who led me to own my story

~ Steven & Larry Strickland, for their honesty, protection, and encouragement

~ My Tribe, who love and support me as I learn to enjoy my ledge view

~ Nancy Erickson, The Book Professor, who coached, edited, and published my story

~ Heidi Kronenberg, ESME.com, for letting my voice be heard

~ Pepper Park Coffee, Lake Barrington, Illinois my happy place, writing spot, and adopted family of cheerleaders

~ Many other old and new friends who held my feet to the flame to bring this book to the finish line by believing that my story has purpose, value, and universal ledge lessons

~ God, always through everything

~ Finally, Reuben W. Strickland, my daddy, who gave me his gift

about the author

A certified professional life coach, **Nancy Jo Nelson** lives in the northwest suburbs of Chicago. Her nest is emptying as her daughter, Jillian, lives in the city and attends North Park University. Her son, Sam, still lives at home, along with Winnie the Wonder Mutt and Bolt the Mighty Chihuahua. *Lessons from the Ledge* is her first book. Visit her website, LedgeLessons.com.

www.ingramcontent.com/pod-product-compliance
Lightning Source LLC
Chambersburg PA
CBHW071347080526
44587CB00017B/3001